Daily Fragrance of the Lotus Flower

Daily Fragrance of the Lotus Flower

Ji Kwang Dae Poep Sa Nim

Volume 3
1994

Bo Duk Religious Research Center
Mountain View, Hawai'i

Energy Spiritual Writing Paintings by Ji Kwang Dae Poep Sa Nim.

Front cover: Title: *"Dragon year: Helping you to have health, a long life, prosperity and peace."* Description: This Year of the Dragon is known as a black or dark Water Dragon Year; historically, it is regarded throughout the Orient and other parts of the world as being difficult and often tumultuous." *Acrylic on canvas.*

Back cover: Title: "World Peace *Kwan Se Um Bo Sal*." Monument at the Lotus Buddhist Monastery in Hawaiʻi. Height: 62 feet tall; made out of solid granite.

First Published in 2012
by Bo Duk Religious Research Center
P. O. Box 787
Mountain View, HI 96771 USA

© 2012 Ji Kwang Dae Poep Sa Nim
ISBN: 978-1-936843-05-3
ISSN: 2159-0869

All rights reserved. No part of this book may be reproduced or transmitted in any form or by any means, electronic or mechanical, including photocopying and recording, or in any information storage or retrieval system, without prior written permission from the publishers.

Author's Opening

Dear Reader,
In the clear, crisp night sky each individual star shines brightly, adorning the heavens with its beauty. The radiance of each star encompasses the whole world and brings forth a beautiful mind for anyone whose gaze takes in the brilliance of the stars, making that person and everyone else happy.

It is just like this: each person is also like one of the bright, shining stars in the beautiful night sky. Without any stars, there is little beauty in the night sky, and the sky itself loses much of its value.

Each individual person is as important as each shining star that gives beauty to all sentient beings. Each person that eliminates his or her impurities by practicing sincerely will become clearer and brighter and ever more radiant. Each practicing person will become like a bright, shining star in the dark sky.

Since July 17, 1992, without missing a single day, through Buddha's message I have been writing the Daily Sutras to help bring out the wisdom that is within each and every one of us.

Each teaching is like a simple reminder that helps you throughout the daily ups and downs of your busy lives, so that in the end you can become like a bright, shining star.

All of the teachings fit the energy of the particular day they are written. Yet, as you read the teachings gathered here, you will see that each and every one of them is actually timeless. These always timely teachings help you by offering beautifully simple ways of understanding and grasping the perplexity of our daily lives as we deal with others, in friendships, in love relationships, in our work, and in pursuing self realization.

As you read these teachings you will see that they are not only for students of Buddhism. They can be applied by anyone, regardless of background, religion, age or gender.

I hope that you enjoy reading these teachings and become your own bright shining star.

Ji Kwang Dae Peop Sa Nim

Foreword

The Daily Fragrance of the Lotus Flower is a comprehensive collection of the daily teachings that have been offered by Ji Kwang Dae Poep Sa Nim, the Supreme Matriarch of the Yun Hwa Denomination of World Social Buddhism, since July 17, 1992. Divided into yearly volumes, this collection is a treasure-store of daily life wisdom. Each teaching is, in truth, a "daily sutra" authored by Ji Kwang Dae Poep Sa Nim in enlightening response to the life issues and questions of Her students and to the shifting complexion of local, national and world events. Whereas the teachings of the historical Buddha — Siddhārtha Gautama or Shakyamuni Buddha — were memorized by His students and passed down orally for generations before being committed to writing, the daily teachings of Ji Kwang Dae Poep Sa Nim have been written by Her own hand, each and every morning, in immediate response to the energy and issues of the day.

This is the second of a precious series of yearly volumes of *The Daily Fragrance of the Lotus Flower* that will be published in an ongoing fashion. Each of the teachings in each volume expresses both the means-to and the meaning-of unblemished clarity and unhindered compassion. As daily sutras, these teachings at once demonstrate enlightened engagement with the relational dynamics of daily life and offer directly useful methods for realizing that there are ultimately no impediments to transforming every situation into the bodhimandala, or "place of enlightenment." Respectfully received and mindfully read, the teachings collected in these volumes are an illumination from within of our ever-changing human situation — a revelation of the suchness (*tathātā*) of daily life and the incomparable and unending path of appreciative and contributory virtuosity.

Social Buddhism

Social Buddhism is the Dharma (Teaching) of daily life wisdom. Social Buddhism is not above sentient beings, and it is not below sentient beings; it is within and together with sentient beings in order to eliminate ignorance and to attain and skillfully enact wisdom.

    The origin of Social Buddhism dates back to the time of Shakyamuni Buddha. The Buddha's recorded teachings (Pali: *suttas*; Sanskrit: *sutras*) reveal the Buddha interacting with and providing wise and compassionate guidance to people from all levels of society — from manual laborers to royalty — in meadows, on mountain peaks, in parks, private homes and palaces. All of these teachings take the form of conversations between the Buddha, his disciples, both ordained and lay students, and people living in the villages, towns and cities that he visited. Most often, the teachings begin with the Buddha being asked a question emerging from the daily life experiences of those fortunate enough to meet him. Thus, from its very beginnings, Buddhism has been socially engaged. Today, Social Buddhism is most thoroughly exemplified by the teachings and practices of the Supreme Matriarch Ji Kwang Dae Poep Sa Nim of the Yun Hwa Denomination of World Social Buddhism. This volume and those to follow collect the Daily Sutras offered by Ji Kwang Dae Poep Sa Nim to Her students and to the rest of the world. They are a treasure house of contemporary daily life wisdom.

Social Buddhism is Omniscient Buddhism and the most encompassing form of Buddhism, embracing teachings and practices from Theravada, Mahayana, Vajrayana and Zen Buddhist traditions. As in other forms of Buddhism, Social Buddhism joins monks and nuns and laypersons through the teachings of Buddha (which means 'the absolute,' 'the truth'), the study of *suttas* or *sutras*, meditation practice, and (as in Zen) the formal teaching of koans (Korean: *kongan*; Chinese: *gongan*). In Social Buddhism, one has to know and honor both the Dharma taught by the Buddha, and the ethical precepts (Vinaya) that inform the Buddhist community (Sangha). But one must also know and honor the customs and manners appropriate in each place and at each time. First and foremost, however, Social Buddhism teaches the means-to and the meaning-of living a correct life every single day, exemplifying a correct mind moment-by-moment.

What distinguishes Social Buddhism from other forms of Buddhism is that the Social Buddhist doctrine is so direct, pure and true (encompassing) that it is able to improvise fluently with the patterns and dynamics of contemporary life, while resolutely guiding people onto the path of Buddha. Unlike traditions that have come to be tightly bound up with specific cultural norms and constrained by fixed paradigms and dogmas rigidly adhered to for centuries, Social Buddhism is flexible enough to respond to people's minds as they have come to be through each person's individual karma, all while following the original Dharma of Shakyamuni Buddha.

In order to have a correct life, one must follow three kinds of practice.

1. Keeping the precepts.
2. Having a meditation mind and dwelling in quietude.
3. Attaining wisdom in order to eliminate ignorance.

If one does not keep the precepts, one's mind becomes hindered and bothered, making it difficult for one to be clear. When one's mind is not in quietude, it is constantly undulating, also rendering one unclear. Finally, dissolving ignorance—the root of trouble and suffering—requires wisdom. That is why these three categories of practice are so important. They are the foundation of Social Buddhism.

While Shakyamuni Buddha was alive, Buddhism most commonly took the form of an ascetic practice reserved for monks and nuns. During the first three-month retreat after Shakyamuni Buddha's *parinirvana* (ultimate release), his students held a Council to recite collectively all the teachings of the Buddha remembered by those present. Roughly 100 years later, a second Council was held to establish a comprehensive canon of the Buddha's teachings. About a half-century later (in the middle of the third century BCE), as a result of disputes about the Vinaya, or rules for monks and nuns, different denominations of Buddhism began to appear.

Mahayana Buddhism began to emerge as a distinct set of teachings and practices about 100 years later in the second century BCE. Over this same period of time, what is now known as Theravada also became established as a distinct tradition. As in the Buddha's original Sangha, Mahayana Buddhism was taught to everyone, regardless of their social status, but still followed the strict ascetic practices associated with Theravada Buddhism. Also, whereas the

Theravada accorded great respect to the *arahants,* or students of the Buddha who realized the meaning of Buddhist practice and liberation, the Mahayana offered greatest reverence to *bodhisattvas,* or beings who dedicate themselves to skillfully-assisting all sentient beings in the realization of liberation.

Although the peoples of Korea may have long had contact with Buddhism through the Silk Roads trade that linked India, Central Asia and East Asia, Mahayana Buddhism was formally introduced to Korea from China by an imperial mission sent during the Korean Goguryeo Dynasty in 372. Buddhism was quickly embraced in Goguryeo and the other kingdoms that existed during the same period on the Korean peninsula, Baekje and Silla. During the Three Kingdoms period, in addition to the Chinese imperial mission that sent Buddhist texts and images to Korea, Korean masters were also traveling to China, bringing back Buddhist teachings.

Buddhism was first formally adopted as a state religion in 529, when the king of Silla officially embraced Buddhism. A court noble named Ichadon was to be executed because of his Buddhist faith. He informed his executioner that to believe in Buddha is the truth, and that as proof of this, white blood would spill from his body once they carried out his execution. White blood did flow from Ichadon's body, and King Beopheung (514–540) was so impressed that he decided to make Buddhism the official state religion of Silla in 529.

From Korea, Buddhism spread to other parts of East Asia, and by the 7th century was well established throughout the region. During the Unified Silla Dynasty, two great masters Uisang (625–702) and Wonhyo (617–686) traveled to Tang Dynasty China and officially brought key Buddhist teachings back to Korea, including the Flower Ornament or Avatamsaka Sutra. Uisang founded the Wonyung (Hwa-eom; Chinese, Huayan) School that has been the foundation for Korean Buddhist doctrinal traditions to the present day. Wonhyo sought to synthesize various Buddhist teachings in an all-inclusive vision and to combine these with Buddhist practices that were effective in daily life as well as in monastic settings.

Bodhidharma, who was the twenty-eighth patriarch in India, exemplified the third form of Buddhism which came to be known as Chan (in China), Zen (in Japan) or Seon (in Korea). Bodhidharma lived during the fifth century. From South India, Bodhidharma traveled to China to see King Wu of the Liang Dynasty (Yan Mun Che) and began to teach Buddhism there, becoming known thereafter as the first patriarch of Chan Buddhism. Before Bodhidharma's arrival, the Chinese studied and practiced various traditions of Mahayana Buddhism, and especially emphasized carrying out bodhisattva actions and building up virtue. King Yan Mu Che was very happy that a great master like Bodhidharma would arrive from India. The king told Bodhidharma that he built many temples, funded Buddhist translation work and did many bodhisattva actions. The king wanted to know how much virtue he had created through all these actions. Bodhidharma told him that he made "no virtue." The king was infuriated and told Bodhidharma, "You said that my virtue is nothing, but you are supposed to be a great master and the twenty-eighth Patriarch. In fact, who are you?" Bodhidharma told the king, "I am nothing." The king did not understand this profound response and the true teaching Bodhidharma was offering to him. Instead, the king only had murderous thoughts, and Bodhidharma left the southeastern coast of China and traveled north to Mount Song (or Sorim Mountain) near the Chinese capital of Luoyang. There he meditated for nine years without once touching the wall with his back to show the value of the practice and the meaning of Zen. Bodhidharma's teaching centered on realizing the one true nature of all things, understanding karma and practicing mindfulness in all situations.

Bodhidharma did not seek students, but one young man named Hea Ga (Huiko) is said to have cut off his arm in the snow to show how much he wanted to learn from Bodhidharma. Bodhidharma decided to teach him, and Hae Ga went on to become recognized as the second patriarch of Zen Buddhism in China. Bodhidharma's lineage became prominent in China with the sixth patriarch, Huineng, who focused on realizing one's own true nature and demonstrating sudden enlightenment or readiness for awakening (*dunwu*). The Chan tradition developed many branches, but enlightened masters like Baizhang, Huangbo, Mazu and Linji came to figure in all the lineages transmitted into Korea and Japan. Chan (Japanese: Zen; Korean: Seon) Buddhism centers on meditation and a special mind-to-mind transmission, beyond words and letters; but Chan also respected the history of Buddhism, attainment of the truth of the sutras and the importance of an enlightened teacher in realizing one's true self. According to Chan, if one does not have clear teaching and guidance, one can easily fall into debilitating vacuity.

Buddhism in Korea went through its most difficult time during the Yi Dynasty (Joseon) (1392–1910), because the dynasty's founder,

King Yi Seong Gye (1335–1408), adopted Confucianism and demoted Buddhism from its position as the national religion. During the earlier Goryeo Dynasty (918–1392), temples were located in villages and were a central part of everyday life. It was not until the Yi Dynasty that temples were forced to move into the mountains. Confucianism existed during the Goryeo Dynasty, but it was not officially recognized as a state religion as in the Joseon.

A key moment for Social Buddhism occurred when the great master Dae Gak Guksa (Uicheon), who was the fourth son of Goryeo Emperor Munjong, traveled to China during the Song Dynasty (1086). Dae Gak Guksa returned from China as a strong advocate of the Cheontae (Chinese: Tiantai; Japanese: Tendai) School, which had adopted the Lotus Sutra as its central scripture. On his return, he established the Cheontae Denomination as a distinct tradition. Cheontae, which quickly became a major, syncretic force in Korean Buddhism, combined an emphasis on meditation (central to Seon/Chan/Zen) and non-duality (central to Hwa-eom/Huayan). It later branched out into several other denominations. Among these new branches was the Poep Hwa Denomination.

Supreme Matriarch Ji Kwang Dae Poep Sa Nim was a student of the Poep Hwa Denomination and eventually received the title of archbishop. Soon thereafter, the Supreme Patriarch of the Poep Hwa Denomination handed down the lineage and Patriarch Kim Gap Yol gave Ji Kwang Dae Poep Sa Nim the title of Supreme Matriarch.

When Supreme Matriarch Ji Kwang Dae Poep Sa Nim came to the West (first to the United States of America and then to Europe), She brought not only the lineage of Cheontae Poep Hwa:

through Her attainment, She realized that global conditions were opportune for revitalizing Shakyamuni Buddha's method of daily teaching in the context of everyday life and for a new flowering of His unbroken lineage of Social Buddhism. To symbolize this, Supreme Matriarch Ji Kwang Dae Poep Sa Nim decided to change the name of Her Cheontae Poep Hwa denomination to Yun Hwa or Lotus Flower. While Poep Hwa means Dharma Flower, the original symbol of Buddhism is the blossoming of the lotus. Supreme Matriarch Ji Kwang Dae Poep Sa Nim is the first Matriarch of the Yun Hwa Denomination of World Social Buddhism.

Social Buddhism has existed since the time of Shakyamuni Buddha. Although Shakyamuni Buddha wanted to teach Social Buddhism, he had to respond to the people living during that period and the quality of their thoughts and mindfulness. Because of their ideologies and concepts, Shakyamuni Buddha had to stress a stricter and more ascetic teaching and practice. Similarly, when Dae Poep Sa Nim first began accepting students in Honolulu, they just wanted good luck and ceremonies, but were not really interested in learning the Dharma. It was not until later, in 1984, when Dae Poep Sa Nim traveled to Europe, that She found students who were open to learning the true Dharma.

During the time of Shakyamuni Buddha, one of His lay students, Vimalakirti, taught a form of Social Buddhism, and Shakyamuni Buddha was very appreciative of that. Shakyamuni Buddha even sent Moon Soo Bodhisattva (Manjusri), the bodhisattva of awareness and wisdom, to attend Vimalakirti. But even Vimalakirti was not able to develop Social Buddhism to its full extent because the mind of the people was inclined more toward ascetic practice.

Social Buddhism is unique in providing the daily life wisdom to perform one's correct function and duties as a human being while also attaining enlightenment. Without going into the mountains and living apart from society, one can live one's daily life and yet also be able to see oneself and reflect upon oneself correctly. One can realize the highest levels of attainment in the very midst of the social world through cultivating true and clear relationships. Social Buddhism is truly boundless.

Supreme Matriarch Ji Kwang Dae Poep Sa Nim is recognized by many to be one of the few masters since Shakyamuni Buddha who has dared to teach and demonstrate what Social Buddhism is by being a living exemplar.

For example, until now, masters and particularly patriarchs or matriarchs always have had to wear formal Dharma robes as part of the Buddhist tradition. The traditional clothing worn by matriarchs and patriarchs is used to show their status and to insure that they receive the proper respect for their attainment. But when Supreme Matriarch Ji Kwang Dae Poep Sa Nim came to Europe, She wore the traditional clothing of a master when She was teaching, but also went beyond the tradition and wore layperson's clothes. Bringing to life the teaching of Chan Master Linji that Buddhist realization means being a "true person of no-rank," Supreme Matriarch Ji Kwang Dae Poep Sa Nim thus demonstrated the bodhisattva meaning of according with every situation and responding as needed. Moment by moment, simply and directly, Her teaching is tirelessly translating the true meaning of Social Buddhism into virtuosic action.

Because of Her great enlightenment, Supreme Matriarch Ji Kwang Dae Poep Sa Nim makes no disparaging differentiations or discriminations among religions or beliefs; everybody and everything is the same, and is part of one world and one universe. This is a truth that has been proclaimed throughout humanity. Social Buddhism teaches that activating the truth of non-duality is realizing that all beings are the same, precisely because they can differ-from and differ-for one another. Through mutual contribution and appreciation, this very situation can become a living paradise.

Secretary Monks
Lotus Buddhist Monastery

Daily Fragrance of the Lotus Flower

Volume 3
1994

"What I am teaching you is not new. You heard about it before in either this or a past life. This daily teaching is simply to remind us so that we can be clear and live correctly in this and future lives. Believing this teaching is entirely the decision of the one who reads it. In addition, applying one's own concept to this teaching is the choice of the reader himself or herself."

— *Ji Kwang Dae Poep Sa Nim*

591. January 1, 1994. Yun Hwa Dharma Sah

Happy New Year!

This is the Year of the Dog. A dog has loyalty-mind. A keen-eyed dog has great loyalty to its master, gives its life to its master and has the nature of a great bodhisattva.

In the animal kingdom, we consider the dog to be one of the highest animals. Dogs have senses similar to the six senses of human beings. A keen-eyed dog, with its great bodhisattva actions, can go directly to paradise (nirvana) without first obtaining a human form.

In this Year of the Dog, let us practice vigorously, let us strive to attain Buddhahood, and let us do many great bodhisattva actions for others. Again, have a happy New Year and let us make others as happy as possible.

This is the year of the fire dog. So let us burn all negativity and suffering, allowing our wisdom to shine like the light of a fire, and let us make the whole world bright with wisdom.

592. January 2, 1994. Yun Hwa Dharma Sah

When you do sitting meditation, sit comfortably, breathe in and out deeply a few times, and repeat the mantra. While repeating the mantra, let your delusions settle down.

When your delusions, thoughts, and also the mantra disappear, when you forget that you are sitting, forget everything, you can see Buddha (the absolute). In Buddha (the absolute), see the no-Buddha. Then, you are not even seeing that no-Buddha, and everything becomes larger, wider and brighter.

In that moment, your body relaxes 100 percent, your mind also relaxes, and everything you see is beautiful. You will feel true happiness; that true happiness will flow into your body and mind, and you can really feel and taste paradise.

At this moment, repeat the mantra, stand up from sitting, and do what you must do at that time.

593. January 3, 1994. Yun Hwa Dharma Sah

Buddha always relays the Dharma to chosen people. Twenty-five hundred years ago, he chose Shakyamuni Buddha and gave the message to him so he could relay it to all sentient beings. Every century, until now, Buddha has chosen some masters to relay the Dharma. It is eternally like this; relaying the Dharma to sentient beings in this way will never change.

The person who is chosen by Buddha must throw away small I and always search for Big I. When one attains Big I, one does not use it for oneself but only for others; that person must even throw away the thinking that he or she is using it for others.

While your form exists, and even after you receive a new one, always make others happy, help them to come out from darkness, lead them to Big I, which is in the realm of Buddha, and help them to become Buddhas themselves.

That kind of purpose and vow must be clear. The person who has that purpose and vow is chosen by Buddha; Shakyamuni Buddha and all previous leaders have been chosen.

594. January 4, 1994. Yun Hwa Dharma Sah

When you make your body stiff, you make this beautiful and bright absolute energy stiff.

When your mind is not honest, you use this beautiful and bright absolute energy crookedly.

When this crooked energy touches others' minds, then they will deal with you in a crooked way.

If you want to receive love and respect from others, make yourself soft. And no matter what situation you are in, do not cheat. Always show yourself honestly. Then, as time goes by, others will deal with you in a true and honest way.

Even though the space which your one body occupies is small, if you can make others comfortable and happy, hundreds and thousands of other people will follow your small body, and the small space that you occupy will become as large as the universe. You will make everyone happy and comfortable, and you will lead them to the realm of Buddha.

595. January 5, 1994. Yun Hwa Dharma Sah

When you listen to others speak, this speech seems to be okay, but so does that one. So you become confused about which speech is really correct.

At that time, do not just follow the correct speech; repeat the mantra and think about the clear and bright realm of Buddha. Then, what is correct will come into your ears and what is incorrect you will forget about. But also forget about that correct speech which comes into your ears and your eyes; forget everything.

Then, when you can see and hear the mantra very clearly, while in the realm of Buddha, you will not get caught by what is correct and what is incorrect. With a comfortable mind, without getting caught by whatever you hear, you can digest everything, and what is correct will become yours. Then you can relay that which is correct to others in a very relaxed and confident way.

This is the way not to influence others negatively and the way to relay the truth to others.

596. January 6, 1994. Yun Hwa Dharma Sah

The body which sat in front of Shakyamuni Buddha twenty-five hundred years ago listening to the Dharma and the body which is sitting here now — are they the same or are they different?

The body which will sit in front of the future Buddha twenty-five hundred years from now, listening to the Dharma, and the body which is sitting here now — are they the same or are they different?

If you say they are the same, you are not correct; and if you say they are different, you are also not correct.

Give me one sentence.

But be careful; do not be a monkey.

In the clear and bright empty mirror, the cold winter wind is fresh and the chanting sound of the wind comes into the ears so clearly.

Putting lips to the warm cup of coffee, those lips make a Dharma speech:

Na Mu Kwan Se Um Bo Sal
Na Mu So Ga Mo Ni Bul
Chong Gak Mio Poep Yun Hwa Kyong

The empty mirror which disappeared is filled with Buddha's smile today.

597. January 7, 1994. Yun Hwa Dharma Sah

In the realm of sentient beings, make truth, goodness and beauty. If you act thus, then the realm of Buddha will recognize you and invite you to the realm of Buddha. It will help you get whatever you want, accomplish whatever you want, and make you completely satisfied. Then, it will give you an important job, such as being an ambassador of the Dharma. You will then be sent back to the realm of sentient beings to show all other sentient beings how to attain and make truth, goodness and beauty; and all of the sentient beings who make truth, goodness and beauty will be like you.

All ambassadors of the Dharma came with an important position and duty. But when they return to the realm of sentient beings, even though they know what their job is, being among other sentient beings leads them to be tainted by the three poisons (desire, anger, ignorance), and so they easily forget their jobs and duties.

This is just like when someone on a long journey is very thirsty and goes to a café for a glass of water. But someone there tells this person that liquor is better than water. While drinking a glass of liquor, this person becomes attached to the taste; one glass becomes two glasses, and two glasses become three glasses. Then this person gets drunk, forgets why he or she is there, falls into confusion and deteriorates.

Always see yourself. Seeing that you are still caught by the three poisons, remove them by practicing. Then you can see clearly why you are here in this world, and you will rediscover your job and duty. Through the actions of making truth, goodness and beauty, you will rediscover yourself, and you will shine for others.

598. January 8, 1994. Honolulu

Whoever you encounter, whether they are good people, negative people or difficult people, always deal with them with the truth.

The original place of all human beings is the truth. But according to the karma one has from the last life or from one's present relationships and situations, one becomes negative, difficult, and sometimes blocked or scared.

But no matter with whom you deal and no matter what kind of relationships and situations you have, if you continuously deal with others with the truth, they will also deal with you with the truth. Having truthful conversations and making truthful actions helps you and others eliminate karma, and helps you make each other into Buddhas and bodhisattvas.

Then, in the truthful realm of Buddha, people will together make truth, goodness and beauty.

599. January 9, 1994. Yun Hwa Dharma Sah

As a wise person's position becomes higher and more important, he or she lowers himself or herself further; taking yet another step, eliminating himself or herself, the wise person finds who he or she is through others.

As unwise people's positions become higher and more important, they put themselves above others and go a step further by wanting to take away others' jobs and by wanting to control everything. When someone is better than they are and does nice things, they become jealous and angry and make others suffer. Finally, they lose everything; and remaining in samsara, in the realm of sentient beings, it is difficult for them to escape suffering.

Always raise the mind of complimenting others and eliminate the mind of complaining about others. The mind which compliments others makes you very respectful, but the mind which complains about others makes you very low and disrespectful.

600. January 10, 1994. Yun Hwa Dharma Sah

In the empty mirror, always see your face. When you look,
- If you have a sad face, fix it to become a happy face.
- If you have an arrogant face, fix it to become a humble face.
- If you have an angry face, fix it to become a face of goodness.
- If you have a jealous face, fix it to become a compassionate face.

Fixing your face actually is the practice. When you fix your face, the Buddha which is reflected in the empty mirror will deal with you with a smile. That smile will make the whole universe smile and will make everyone happy.

A person who makes others happy is able to come out from the realm of sentient beings and can live in the realm of Buddha, without suffering. But because that person wants to make sentient beings happy, he or she returns to the realm of sentient beings and leads them all to the realm of Buddha, everyday.

601. January 11, 1994. Yun Hwa Dharma Sah

Those who practice for nothingness become more famous after they die and are eternally famous.

Those who practice for somethingness become famous while alive, but after they die, others make many complaints about them.

Nothingness is infinite truth; somethingness is temporary, impermanent truth.

Something, which comes from nothingness, returns to nothingness. But nothing, which comes from nothingness, always stays in nothingness.

When those who realize the meaning of nothingness are in difficulty, they know how to make that difficulty into happiness. But when those who are caught by somethingness are in difficulty, they make that difficulty into more difficulty.

602. January 12, 1994. Yun Hwa Dharma Sah

Today is the first of the month by the lunar calendar, so give others a lot of love.

Even if there is someone you do not like, give him or her lots of love.

Even if there is someone who is difficult for you, give him or her lots of love.

Love everybody today. Today is love day.

603. January 13, 1994. Yun Hwa Dharma Sah

When you are disappointed, do not blame the situation for your disappointment, and do not try to cover up that you are disappointed.

Throw your disappointment away and look for the true cause of your disappointment.

You can then realize that the cause came from you. At that time, do not blame yourself. Just forget about everything. Strive to polish yourself, and try to be as clear as possible so that you do not have to experience that kind of disappointment again. Your striving will bring you happiness in the future, and the disappointment that you had will make you a master of yourself.

604. January 14, 1994. Yun Hwa Dharma Sah

A boat is moved by the water currents; a kite is moved by wind currents. If a boat defies water currents and does not flow with them, or if a kite defies wind currents and does not follow them, then they wreck themselves.

As human beings proceed on their paths, the right situations, the right opportunities and the right relationships always appear. When they appear, do not defy them; follow them. If you defy them, you lose everything. But if you follow them, you earn everything.

An unawakened person tries to find happiness from far away. But an awakened person encounters happiness right in front of his or her eyes and nose.

605. January 15, 1994. Yun Hwa Dharma Sah

When the mind is clean, everything looks beautiful, and no matter what situation you are in, everything is comfortable. It is just like being in paradise.

When the mind is complicated, everything looks complicated, and no matter what situation you are in, everything seems to be difficult.

Clear mind is Buddha's mind; complicated mind is sentient being's mind.

In a single day, mind changes many times between being Buddha's mind and being sentient being's mind. See your mind many times each day; see how much dust (desire, anger, ignorance) there is, and always practice to clean your mind. Then you can make this world a paradise, live a paradisiacal life and accomplish becoming a Buddha.

And that Buddha will live everyday with a smile.

606. January 16, 1994. Yun Hwa Dharma Sah

Today is the day of the boat ceremony. On this day, we offer love and food to Buddha, nature, and our ancestors.

So today you should be tranquil, try not to think, and be yourself. Appreciate the existence of life and the fact that you can make this kind of offering to Buddha, nature, and the ancestors. Your offering karma will then last forever, and you will always be protected by Buddha, nature, and the ancestors.

607. January 17, 1994. Yun Hwa Dharma Sah

The closer your relationship with someone becomes, the more you should respect and protect one another; also, you should deal with one another as you did when you first met. Then that relationship will be beautiful for eternity.

When you first meet someone, you do not show your conditions because you want to begin a relationship. But afterwards, the closer you become, the more your own conditions appear and the more you wish for the other to abide by your conditions. But being in a relationship means making the other happy.

So do not irritate others because of your own conditions.

608. January 18, 1994. Yun Hwa Dharma Sah

From the time human beings are born until they die, they always carry a heavy sack on their backs. In that sack are the three poisons (desire, anger and ignorance), the five desires (for food, fame, sex, sleep and money), jealousy, and the eight sufferings. They always carry this sack, and because they think it is a precious jewel, they are always covering and protecting it, thus making it heavier and heavier.

But when they meet the Dharma and teachings, they one by one unload the contents of the sack. Often, while unloading these things, they suffer because there is a conflict between small I and Big I. Small I thinks that what is inside of the sack is precious, but Big I thinks that what is inside is not.

Through continuous practice, Big I wins and comfortably removes, one by one, everything that is inside of the sack. The sack is gradually emptied, and people realize that what was inside was nothing but garbage. So they even throw the sack away.

At that time, on their shoulders, just where the sack had been, there sits a Dharma bird, and those people sit upon a blooming lotus flower. Wherever they go, a bright light shines and they eliminate darkness. All sentient beings follow those people and relax comfortably in the realm of Buddha.

609. January 19, 1994. Yun Hwa Dharma Sah

The parrot who speaks well does not know the intention of the dog who cannot speak well; but the dog knows that the parrot is only talking without its speech meaning anything.

Be just like a dog who knows everything and not like a parrot; and do your practice. Then you will be able to deal with a talking parrot without getting hurt, and you will also know how to take care of people who, like dogs, do not speak too much.

610. January 20, 1994. Honolulu

Repeat the mantra:

Na Mu Kwan Se Um Bo Sal,
Na Mu So Ga Mo Ni Bul,
Chong Gak Mio Poep Yon Hwa Kyong.

Repeat it as much as you can, ten thousand or one hundred thousand times.

Then everything will settle, and what is in front of your eyes will become clear and bright.

This mantra is guiding you to the correct path of life and, at the same time, is helping you accomplish what you must do.

Na Mu Kwan Se Um Bo Sal,
Na Mu So Ga Mo Ni Bul,
Chong Gak Mio Poep Yon Hwa Kyong.
Na Mu....

611. January 21, 1994. Honolulu

When you know love, love is very important and it creates happiness, beauty, and all things.

When you do not know love, everything becomes dry, is made into suffering, and many things are eliminated.

To know and receive love, we must first know how to love others. Do not discriminate between good- looking and bad-looking; and love unconditionally. At that time you can save yourself from the hard shell of suffering.

To do that, practice the mantra. Unconditional love comes from the practice of the mantra; the mantra will show you what love is and how to create it.

612. January 22, 1994. Honolulu

When you take strong medicine, your mind becomes "bong." You hallucinate, and you cannot remember what you did, said, or thought.

It is the same thing when you are caught in strong karma: your actions, speech and thinking are not clear, and because of this you also make others unclear and confused.

So before you give your opinion to others, first check to see if you are clear and if your opinion will hurt others. Check that, and practice not to make others suffer because of your own self.

613. January 23, 1994. Honolulu

In the place of unclarity, true I is always watching you. To discover true I in the place of unclarity is very difficult. But the mind which really wants to strive and practice to discover true I will discover it, and will depart from unclarity. Then you will find true I, true direction, and will again go onto the correct path.

In this world there are many situations which are just like hallucinations. If at those times you know that you are hallucinating, you do not have to worry. The mind which knows that it is hallucinating will always help lead you to the discovery of true I, and will help you realize that hallucinations are nothing but phantoms.

Those of you who have had drug experiences should always remember that your truth is always watching you and that it wants you to find your true self. So do not indulge in hallucinations, which are only phantoms and dreams.

Your true I is the only place where you can greatly relax, have a healthy body and have true happiness, which words cannot express. So while going on the path of your life, do not let anyone hinder or interrupt you, no matter how tempting it may be. And no matter how difficult that may sometimes be, go through it. Then you will find true paradise, which means true nirvana, in this present life.

614. January 24, 1994. Honolulu

When you are not clear and someone speaks, it sounds as if that person is complaining about you.

When you are not clear and someone laughs, it sounds as if that person is belittling you.

When you are not clear and someone compliments you, it sounds as if that person is twisting it around.

When you are not clear, everything you hear makes you angry, depressed and disappointed. This means that you are in the small

I, but you want to deny it; and you become confused because you think you are in the Big I. Because you think that you are in the Big I, you wish for no one to bother you and you overprotect yourself.

The person who is very arrogant overprotects himself, always feeling that he or she is the best, and does not want to admit that they are still in the small I. That is why they cannot truthfully accept things and always turn white into black. That puts them into the shell of small I, and from there it is difficult to go onto the path of Big I.

People like this should first practice not to be bothered by anything, whether someone complains about them or compliments them; whatever it is, they should just forget it. Then they can truthfully distinguish between what is right and what is wrong.

When you deal with this kind of person, actions are better than speech, until his ears correctly open.

615. January 25, 1994. Honolulu

The space of the universe is wide and great. But nowadays human beings' mind space is becoming smaller and smaller. People do not want to listen to or understand others' ideas; they only want to voice their own opinions and have others tell them that only they are right. When others do not listen to them, they become angry and from their lips there exudes the unpleasant smell of bad speech — speech that makes others feel bad.

This comes from people's attachment to life and their unsettled daily lives. Their mind of attachment to life comes from their not knowing what true I is, and their unsettled lives come from their following karma I.

The reason we practice is to find our true I, so that we can return our karma I to it. So while you practice and you have a bad feeling because of others, remember this teaching. Do not make yourself feel bad and do not blame others. Even if others' actions and speech are ridiculous, strive to listen to and understand them. In so striving, you will be comfortable, and your comfortably relaxed actions will help to eliminate others' anger and their cramped mind space. And at the same time, you will make one another happy.

616. January 26, 1994. Honolulu

While we practice, it seems that we understand and that once in a while we see the bright and clear realm of Buddha. We then want to retain this bright and clear realm of Buddha and abide in it all day long.

In the morning, you promise yourself that you want to stay in the realm of Buddha, all day. Then you leave your house. But by the time you return home, you have forgotten about the realm of Buddha, and you only bring disappointment and anger with you. You struggle to digest it all, but that does not happen right away. So you keep trying to settle it and you practice once again in order to see the realm of Buddha. This, actually, is practice.

When you do this over and over again, continuously, as time passes by you can stay and live in the realm of Buddha, without being hindered, distracted, disturbed or attacked by anyone.

617. January 27, 1994. Honolulu

In the battle of the survival of the fittest, it is very difficult to sacrifice oneself and help others. But when you do those most difficult things, you become a bodhisattva and a Buddha. If you fail to do those most difficult things and only do things for yourself, it is difficult to depart from the realm of sentient beings and to eliminate suffering; you always live difficultly.

Both of these ways of conducting yourself in the battle for survival are difficult. Please think about which is most worthwhile for you. Think about it!

Surviving is difficult. But if you do what is difficult correctly, difficulty disappears, and you can live in a very appreciative and happy way.

But there is one thing you never have to have difficulty or suffering with, that you can always live happily with. Give me one sentence about what that is. Send me a fax or a letter!

618. January 28, 1994. Honolulu

Always strive to live brightly and clearly, and to have no dark clouds in your mind. But when dark clouds do appear in your mind, strive to transform them in brightness and clarity.

While striving to do so, it is difficult. But just as after lots of rain and thunder, the dark clouds that have covered the sky disappear and the sun shines brightly, in time the dark clouds in your mind dissipate.

So when you are always striving, even if a dark cloud appears, it disappears right away. In the beginning, it is difficult; but when you continuously strive, even the darkest clouds cannot come near you, and you can continuously live a bright and clear life.

When you are in a negative situation or have negative feelings, forget them as soon as possible.

619. January 29, 1994. Honolulu

나옴 관세옴 보살
나옴 옴가모니불
헝강호법 e화형

When you repeat this mantra:
1)   Do not speak badly to others.
When you repeat this mantra:
2)   Do not speak badly about others.
When you repeat this mantra:
3)   Do not disparage others.
When you repeat this mantra:
4)   Do not make others angry.
When you repeat this mantra:
5)   Do not be sycophantic towards others.
When you repeat this mantra:
6)   Do not be jealous of others.

When you repeat this mantra:

7) Do not try to show that you are smarter than others.

When you follow these principles, this mantra becomes a great guiding light for you; it becomes a great protector for you, makes you into a bodhisattva and a Buddha. And it makes you eternally happy, for sure.

620. January 30, 1994. Honolulu

Whatever your general thinking and plans are, check them today. Are those plans and thoughts only for your own benefit? Are they bothering or hurting others? Try checking.

If your plans and thoughts are bothering or hurting others, reduce them by 50 percent. And if your plans and thoughts are only for yourself, change them. Then, instead of bothering or hurting others, those plans and thoughts will turn around; they will help others, and you will be able to realize how small and petty you have been.

Keep your mind open and wide like a vast, shoreless ocean. But when you use your mind, use it like the tip of a needle.

621. January 31, 1994. Honolulu

Do not release anger with anger.

Do not release jealousy with jealousy.

Do not release resentment and grudges with resentment and grudges.

Release anger by being tranquil and serene.

Release jealousy by offering.

Release resentment and grudges by being compassionate.

Never think faraway thoughts. Always remember and think that Buddha is in front of your eyes and nose.

Then, anger does not appear, jealousy does not appear, and resentment and grudges do not appear.

P. S. *This is a very important formula. Repeat it several times, so that it goes into your head.*

622. February 1, 1994. Honolulu

Ten thousand things come out from tranquility and ten thousand things go back to tranquility.

When there is a strong noise, that noise also goes back to tranquility.

The truth is in tranquility; you cannot find the truth in noise. If an idea appears from tranquility, then that idea is coming from the truth. But if an idea appears from noise, then it is nothing but an opinion which cannot connect with anyone and which transmits nothing but noise.

As a person who is seeking for the truth, you should always put yourself into tranquility, find Buddha in tranquility, and do bodhisattva action in tranquility.

623. February 2, 1994. Honolulu

When you have a bad situation, do not become angry and disappointed because of it, and do not blame the person who seems to have caused you to have that bad situation.

Change your thinking. Think of your bad situation as a teaching for you and as occurring for you, not against you. When you think about your bad situation in a good way, it changes into a good situation which will become better and better.

Once you realize this, when you have a bad situation, you will not collapse because of it and you will be able to eliminate your disappointment. Then, no matter how difficult your situation is, you will know how to pass through it right away and will be able to spend every day as a good day.

624. February 3, 1994. Honolulu

Meditation is not only sitting. Whether you are walking, standing, sitting or lying down, as long as the mind is not scattered all around, that is meditation. Especially when you can meditate while going about your daily activities — that is meditation during which you can see yourself in the empty mirror.

Always put the mind into one place and make correct speech, correct thinking and correct action. That meditation is truthful meditation.

When you act while in truthful meditation, your action does not bother others, it does not result in memories for you, and it does not leave any traces for yourself. Because you forget everything, you will not be hindered by what you did.

The un-scattered mind is just like a great, quiet ocean in which no storms appear. In it there is nothing but beautiful waves, and so even small boats without a sail can go comfortably upon it.

625. February 4, 1994. Honolulu

Human beings' power is limited. No matter how hard they try, sometimes what they try to do does not work out, and no matter how good their ideas are, they sometimes do not connect with others.

But there is a power beyond the human power which cannot be seen with the eyes and which cannot be grasped with the hands. There is also wisdom which cannot be realized through thinking. That wisdom is Buddha's absolute penetration power. You can only attain this power through the path of practice and by being in the Dharma.

When you follow the Dharma (the teachings) and the practice, and when you have confidence in the Dharma (the teachings) and the practice, that confidently believing mind becomes one with Buddha's absolute penetration power. Then, the more you try, the more successful you become.

In no-thinking, wisdom appears — a wisdom that handles everything beautifully, connects with others and creates true beauty.

626. February 5, 1994. Honolulu

To relax sounds easy, but it is not. Most body and mind sicknesses come from not being relaxed. So in everyday life, if you can really relax for even ten minutes a day, you can have a healthy life.

Human life is often just like a chase. Try to stop chasing after things, and once in a while, relax. The method for relaxation is not to think about oneself for at least ten minutes a day. During those ten minutes, think about others and do actions in which you sacrifice yourself for others. Then you can really relax.

So relax today!

627. February 6, 1994. Honolulu

Check yourself today and see how recalcitrant and hard-headed you are. Recalcitrance can sometimes protect you, but at other times it can ruin you.

Recalcitrance comes from small I in which one believes that only one's own opinions are correct, and in which one is very self-righteous. This comes from an unwise place. Recalcitrance always generates recalcitrance; it separates you from true I, makes blockages between yourself and others, makes enemies, and leads to harm.

Wise people are not recalcitrant. They always know how to listen to others' opinions, how to understand others, and they can deal with and take care of everything in a round way that does not leave any traces.

628. February 7, 1994. Honolulu

Nowadays, nature is changing a lot. During this time of change, if you want to protect yourself, you must also change. You must change your karma, habits and thinking.

In order to change your karma, habits and thinking correctly, you must realize true I, which is non-discriminating I. In other words, you must realize the equality of all sentient beings. You must realize that, and how all we sentient beings are connected with one another. When someone else is happy, we are happy; and when someone else is sad, we are sad. This means that we are not separate from one another. If we take care of others as we do ourselves, and if we understand others as we do ourselves, we can realize true I.

Change yourself to be better-connected with others. This way we can all protect one another, and no matter how much nature changes, we will not be hindered by it.

So reflect today upon your old karma, habits and thinking, and if there is anything in them that distances or disconnects you from others, forget it.

629. February 8, 1994. Honolulu

When you practice and reach a certain level, you seem to become sensitive to everything; everything seems to bother you, and it seems that you become more negative than before. You also suddenly become lonelier.

This is the process of eliminating your karma and old habits. When you pass that stage, suddenly everything becomes positive and you have confidence in everything, just as if you had already become a Buddha.

At that time, you must be careful and strive not to let your ego grow. After you pass that stage, everything settles and you can find true equanimity and tranquility. In tranquility, you will take care of everything and handle things beautifully, one by one; the non-fragrant fragrance will perfume your surroundings, and you will not incite or irritate others, but instead make them happy and comfortable.

630. February 9, 1994. Honolulu

During the night, sleep with Buddha (truth, absolute).

In the morning, get up with Buddha.

During the day, work within Buddha's embrace.

If you do not forget for even a single minute that you are in Buddha, you do not have to doubt about your path of life; fears do not appear, greed does not appear, and anger does not appear. Also, ignorance disappears. You can see everything correctly, you can think correctly, and you can act correctly.

631. February 10, 1994. Honolulu

Happy New Year!

Today is the lunar New Year. Throughout this year, I wish for you all not to have any problems, to be healthy, for all your wishes to come true, to be wealthy, to be satisfied, and to have great happiness.

The earth revolves around the sun, and the moon revolves around the earth, thus making *yin* and *yang* energy. According to *yin* and *yang* energy, everything is created. But in the human mind there is something which is not affected by *yin* and *yang* energy.

That something is connected with the true mind and true I. When you find that something, you are not affected or hindered by *yin* or *yang*, joy or sadness, happiness or unhappiness, good or bad, beauty or ugliness. That something transcends discrimination and lives a truly happy life. And according to the time, place and connections, that something can make *yin* and *yang* energy and balance it, can make everything comfortable and tranquil.

This new year I want you to find that something. Please practice regularly, find that something, and bring it to next year's New Year's Eve party!

632. February 11, 1994. Honolulu

When you realize Buddha's world, the four and ten directions all open and not even one place is blocked. If you realize this, then no matter where you go, wherever your footsteps carry you is your house, and whoever you meet is your family; you never feel like a stranger and you are always happy to see them.

But human beings' karma makes the mind narrow and separates our one country into many countries and our one family into billions of families. So people always fight and argue: "this is mine," "that is yours," "I am better than you are," "you are lesser than me," etc. It is pitiful.

But when you realize that this whole world is one country and one family, narrow mind disappears, karma disappears; and everyone becomes Buddha's bright I, takes care of and helps each other as one family. Arguing and fighting also disappear, and everyone does bodhisattva action and beautifully adorns this Buddha land.

Let us practice vigorously so that we may come out from our karma as soon as possible and attain Buddha's unblocked and non-hindered world.

633. February 12, 1994. Los Angeles

When Buddha's eyes see human beings, it is very interesting what each of us receives through our actions, one after the other.

For example, a person who is always angry always draws anger from others.

A person who is always sad always elicits sadness from others.

A person who always blames others is always blamed by others.

A person who is always jealous is always regarded jealously by others.

A person who is always very picky is always shunned by others.

A person who only thinks of himself does not receive credit from others.

A person who is dishonest is always mistrusted by others.

But a person who is honest is always respected by others.

When you act, please see yourself correctly, with Buddha's eyes, and act correctly so you can live a correct life. This is not difficult to do; the path of correct living is always present in each moment.

634. February 14, 1994. Paris

In this tranquil realm of Buddha, if insisting upon one's rights and going for one's own benefit hurts others, it makes this tranquil realm of Buddha noisy and dirty.

But if insisting on your rights shows compassion for others, and if going for your own benefit benefits others, though at first it seems to make this tranquil realm of Buddha noisy and dirty, this tranquil realm of Buddha will develop a fragrance of the Dharma which will envelope you, and this tranquil realm of Buddha will softly undulate with love.

Happy Valentine's Day!!

635. February 15, 1994. Paris

Come out from the realm of Buddha, do Buddha's duty, and then go back into the realm of Buddha.

But, what does it mean that even though you come out from the realm of Buddha, you do not know what Buddha is; even though you act as a Buddha, you do not know what Buddha's action is, and even though you go back into the realm of Buddha, you do not know that you are going back into the realm of Buddha?

It means you are making the realm of Buddha dirty, putting yourself into the karmic whirlpool, and making yourself a sentient being. Doing so, it is very difficult to rescue oneself from the wheels of samsara.

Try to remember the first paragraph. Then you will be clear about your direction and path.

636. February 16, 1994. Paris

In the world aflame with greed, keep the mind like a tranquil ocean.

To angry sentient beings, offer compassion.

To sentient beings who act ignorantly, give unlimited love.

If you do these things, that is Buddha doing his correct duty. Because Buddha wants everyone to become a Buddha, he turns the wheel of samsara himself and appears here and there.

Today is a day of endurance. Endure all difficulty and conquer all difficulty. The power which you get from conquering difficulty will vanquish karma I and lead you to find true I.

Remember, true success comes after difficulty. So endure as much as you can and think of this endurance as the beauty of life.

637. February 17, 1994. Paris

When you settle your mind, you can eliminate your problems, one by one.

The method to settle your mind is having faith in the Dharma, the absolute and the teachings. That faithfulness will settle your mind, just like dipping a dirty body into the water and washing the dirt away, one part at a time.

So dip your body into the tranquil Dharma and wash your dirt away, one part at a time, with the teachings. Then your clean body and mind become one with Buddha, and wherever you go you will spread the fragrance of the lotus flower.

The blue mountain wants me to live without speaking and the blue sky wants me to live without any dirt. They want me to live without greed and anger, to live like wind and flowing water.

638. February 18, 1994. Paris

Human knowledge is always limited.

Humans' opinions are always unlimited.

When there is a problem and you ask one person for the solution, you are told to do it this way; when you ask another person, you are told to do it another way. You do not know which one is correct and so you suffer and have a dilemma.

At that time:

Put everything down and do not go in search of right and wrong.

Only think about Buddha (absolute, truth) and do not let that thinking have any dust.

Think about the bright and clear Buddha, and repeat the mantra.

After repeating the mantra, make a wish for yourself to go onto the correct path. Then, forget about it.

Then in the near future the correct path will appear, and without thinking or doubting, you will just act and enter it. This is the independent and wise life.

639. February 19, 1994. Paris

With an angry mind, everything seems to be angry, like a raging fire, and it makes others suffer.

With a tranquil mind, everything is tranquil, and if you see fire or anger you do not get caught by them, but simply put out the flames in a tranquil way.

Even for those who have a lot of karma, if they practice and attain a tranquil mind, one morning they will become Buddhas.

Whenever you are angry and desirous, extinguish anger and desire by yourself; do not let them out; strive to eliminate them by their roots. If even one wrong sentence comes out of your mouth, it creates a seed which will become karma and make you suffer.

Always put everything into the quiet tranquility. Become a Buddha yourself. And if others make mistakes, with Buddha's eyes forgive them compassionately and then put yourself back into tranquility. Attain the realm of Buddha and do not let any dust enter.

This is the great, unhindered, free life.

640. February 20, 1994. Paris

When those who have attained the truth stay with others, they do not irritate them, and though they are present with others, it seems as though they are not even there. When they work, they do not conflict with others and work diligently; when they relax, they make others comfortable and relaxed. People who are like this have already thrown away I, my and me. They only live for others and are true bodhisattvas. Whoever is able to recognize and appreciate these people is also a bodhisattva.

When you make others comfortable, you become comfortable. But when you bother others, you also are bothered. Doing the former and not the latter is easy enough to understand. But it is difficult to accomplish. Still, try doing so.

Food which has no taste is medicine for the body. But food which has taste easily becomes poison.

So become a tasteless but useful person.

641. February 21, 1994. Paris

A person who is untruthful and chases the rainbow meets, connects with and stays with untruthful people who chase rainbows.

A truthful person meets, connects with and stays with truthful people.

The kind of people you meet, connect with and stay with before beginning to practice are not the same as those that you will meet, connect with and stay with as you begin practicing, and as your practice deepens. Also, it can happen that while you practice you meet people you knew before, but you no longer feel comfortable with them and feel lonely.

But at that time, do not worry about being lonely. This loneliness is helping to eliminate your karma, so when you feel like this, practice even harder.

When your practice becomes deep and you find your true I, however, loneliness disappears; wherever you go and whoever you meet, whether they are good or bad, connected or not connected with you, you are not bothered by them, and everyone is just like your friends, family, brothers and sisters. You feel comfortable with whoever you meet and at the same time you make them comfortable. Whoever you are connected with is truthful to you.

642. February 22, 1994. Paris

In Buddha's eyes, everything looks lovely and all sentient beings look beautiful. But when sentient beings suffer, it hurts Buddha and he suffers, too.

It is just like when a small child gets hurt: his mother suffers and her mind is not comfortable until her child's injury has healed. This is why Buddha suffers more than sentient beings and why he has great sadness, which is great compassion.

Until all sentient beings become comfortable, Buddha will not be comfortable. When all sentient beings become Buddhas and are comfortable, then Buddha also will be comfortable.

Let us think deeply about the meaning of this. With this teaching you should know that your practice is not just for yourself but for everyone, that it will make Buddha comfortable, and that Buddha's comfort is also your own.

643. February 23, 1994. Paris

You promise yourself that you will not be greedy. But when something appears that you like, you become greedy and try to satisfy your greed.

But when your body suddenly becomes sick and situations do not work out as you would like, you check yourself and ask why this happens. The first thing that appears in your mind is, "I was so greedy, and that is why I have this problem now."

You promise yourself that you will not be greedy again, but you again break your promise. You keep on promising yourself, you keep on having regrets, and you keep on realizing. But some day, when the time is ripe, there is nothing to regret and nothing to realize. Then you will not be caught or hindered by anything, and you will live a free life.

644. February 24, 1994. Paris

The path of the true, absolute Buddha is wide open in the four and ten directions; it is not blocked.

But the path of the human mind is very limited, small, blocked and closed. So humans suffer a lot, and while going along on their path, they often make wrong turns and waste their time. The reason for this is that they do not seek the path of the true, absolute Buddha, choosing instead the path of satisfying their own desires, greed and comfort.

But if they throw away that which is only for themselves, choosing the path of benefiting and satisfying others, even though there will be times when going on this path seems difficult and blocked, the path will always open, and they will be able to proceed on the path of the true, absolute Buddha. They can then accomplish whatever they want, and wherever they go, it will always have a great purpose.

645. February 25, 1994. Vienna

Life is coming empty-handed, going empty-handed; coming all alone, and going all alone. That is life.

But if when you get a small thing you know how to be satisfied by it, and if when you are with someone else you know to appreciate that person, then even though you come empty-handed, wealth and prosperity will follow you; even though you go by yourself, everyone will respect you and follow in your footsteps.

Then, life after life, you will always prosper and be wealthy. You will come without loneliness, you will live without loneliness, and you will go without loneliness.

646. February 26, 1994. Vienna

When you are reflected in the bright and clear mirror, first you can see your appearance; second, you can see the darkness of your appearance; third, you can see the worry in your appearance; and fourth, you can see, in your appearance, that you are running away from something.

But first, view what you see as Buddha; second, view what you see as being bright and clear; third, view what you see as being happy; and fourth, view what you see as being comfortable. Then, let all appearances disappear, become one with the mirror, and then look again at what you see.

What do you see?

P. S. This is a magical teaching.

647. February 27, 1994. Vienna

When you stay with people who always complain about and demean others, you feel very uncomfortable. When you are with such people, do not try fighting with them. Give yourself space from them until you have the wisdom to convince them and guide them correctly.

The reason you are uncomfortable with people who always complain and demean others is that they make you dizzy and unclear, and you end up making unnecessary karma for yourself because of them.

While taking space from them, remember that everything that appears later disappears into emptiness. When you attain this, you will not be hindered by others; and at the same time, you will have the wisdom to truly understand them. Then, without fighting and becoming dirty, you can make others comfortable and help save them from their negativity.

648. February 28, 1994. Paris

When your body is tired and you want to rest but your thinking is not tired, you have more thinking and you cannot rest. Because that thinking cannot distinguish between day time and night time, it makes the body more tired.

Many people take medicines and liquors in order to rest, but then the next day they feel more tired because of them. People would like to forget about their thinking and put it down, but the more one wants to put it down, the more strongly it appears.

At that time, do the mantra and tell yourself, "I will think about everything tomorrow. In this moment, I am within Buddha's embrace, I am covered with Buddha's blanket, and I will sleep with Buddha." Repeat this sentence several times; then your thinking will disappear and you will be able to rest.

That mind which thinks you are within Buddha's embrace is Buddha; that thinking which wants to be with Buddha cuts off other thoughts; and that thinking which covers yourself with Buddha's blanket makes you forget and put everything down, makes you become one with Buddha's mind, and allows you to rest without hindrance.

649. March 1, 1994. Paris

Delusion appears and disappears like a cloud in the bright and clear sky.

Each time delusion appears, the six senses and five desires appear, and together they cause confusion. When delusion relaxes, the six senses and five desires relax. After delusion disappears, when that no-mind is clear and shines brightly, the six senses and five desires discover their own duties and perform their correct functions.

At that time, the six senses become a Buddha and the five desires become a great bodhisattva.

650. March 2, 1994. Paris

While your mind is quiet, a thought suddenly appears and you try to follow it. But then another thought appears which says, "That other thought is not correct. It is making others suffer and is an ugly thought."

The second thought wants to eliminate the first thought. But the first thought does not want to lose and so it says to the second thought, "No! You are not correct." Then the second thought replies to the first thought, "You are only for yourself. That is why you make many mistakes and why you make others suffer. You are making a lot of bad karma and I cannot agree with you. Through practice I realize that whatever is only for myself is not correct. So I do not trust you anymore. Please get out!"

At that time the first thought disappears, and then the second thought disappears too. The mind becomes quiet again, and, without realizing it, you get up from the chair and the first words you say to others are, "How may I help you? I want to make you happy and comfortable."

651. March 3, 1994. Paris

Sometimes it seems that those who practice, who know what practice is and have received many teachings, are improving. But if their speech and actions are not clear, their speech and actions poke and hurt others. Because they are not clear, others do not listen to or support their explanations, and this leads these people to complain about others for not listening to or supporting their unclear ideas.

People like this always talk about the past, recalling, for example, how someone disappointed them a long time ago. But their being disappointed was not the other person's fault; it was actually their own fault. Even so, because they have been disappointed, they do not trust this other person and until today blame him or her for having hurt them in the past.

Is this the correct speech and action for a practitioner and for one who claims to know the path? When you say that you are disappointed by others, and when you complain about others, that means that you are not clear. You must realize that.

Strive to be clear so that you do not poke others or hurt their feelings. And when you are clear, the person who disappointed you will respect and follow you. Until that time, wait patiently and do not blame others.

Clear people speak briefly, and it is because their brief speech is clearly connected with others that they do not have to talk for a long time. But unclear people talk a lot and for a long time. And because their long speech is not connected with others, when they talk they make others' minds unclear. The degree to which they cause others to be unclear is the degree to which they become unclear in turn. People like this are wasting others' time and energy.

So practice people, when you speak, speak clearly, without poking or bothering others. And practice to speak in ways that make others happy. When your speech makes others happy, your karma of being disappointed by others and of blaming others will disappear.

652. March 4, 1994. Barcelona

If you throw a stone into the quiet ocean which says nothing, which flows quietly, and which makes everyone very comfortable, and you then claim the ocean is rough, the ocean is angry, and the ocean is not blue, how ignorant is your blaming of the ocean?

In everything, what you do is what you get. Whatever kind of seed you plant is what grows. If you complain that you do not have a good situation, a comfortable life, or happiness, then that is all because of what you made yourself.

Do not complain about the results. See the causes. If there is a wrong cause, fix it immediately. If you find in the causes of a situation your own ego, your own efforts to show off, and your lack of respect for others, then the future result cannot be other than complaints and disappointment.

When you know the cause and there is something wrong in it, fix it. Then after you fix it, forget about everything and go without saying anything, becoming like the quiet ocean. Then happiness will fill the ocean.

653. March 5, 1994. Barcelona

We human beings live in love and compassion, but we do not attain what love and compassion truly are; that is why we have difficulty performing our correct functions and duties. But when you realize love and compassion, you can perform your correct functions and duties; you are unhindered and uncaught by your karma, and you can live a free, liberated life.

Our bodies and minds are made from love and compassion. So when our bodies and minds attain love and compassion, they become one with love and compassion, and they are able to offer love and compassion to others, helping them realize what love and compassion are.

What are love and compassion?

I will tell you when the stone-bird mother who lives in the south flies north to feed her baby stone bird. At that time, I will tell you.
P. S. What does the above kong-an mean?

654. March 6, 1994. Barcelona

Think about other people's grandparents as your own grandparents.

Think about other people's parents as your own parents.

Think about other people's children as your own children.

If you think about others' families as your own family, you do not make a separation between yourself and others. Then you can also respect and help others' families as your own family, and you will not have any blockages with others.

The mind which thinks of others' families as one's own family is Buddha's mind, and your action of helping others' families as your own family is bodhisattva action.

All sentient beings in the world are your family. Your direct family becomes your direct family because of a karmic connection you have with them from last life. That is the only difference between direct and non-direct family. So even a stranger whom you meet only for a brief moment once or twice this life can become your direct family next life.

If you care for others' families, you will always have a great family, and you will live happily and appreciatively, life after life.

655. March 7, 1994. Paris

After you realize what love and compassion are, angry mind disappears, disappointed mind disappears, and blaming mind disappears. That mind which was angry then gives others space, makes them comfortable and helps them realize their own mistakes; that mind which was disappointed then understands others more clearly, and so you do not want to do what others do not want you to do. That mind which blamed others then wants to make others better than oneself, and so it watches and protects them.

You will also thoroughly realize that all sentient beings are yourself, and that you are them. So you will not want to make others angry, you will not want to disappoint them, and you will not want to blame them. You will know that their happiness is your happiness.

656. March 8, 1994. Paris

There is a saying from a long time ago: "Cover your eyes and then say 'meow.'" The meaning of this is that in front of certain people, such as one who is higher than you, a person who needs you, your boss or your master, you do things very well. But as soon as you are no longer in front of those people, you think that you are the boss and are higher than others. So you boss others around and try to make yourself comfortable. But people soon discover how sycophantic and ignorant you are.

Clear people do not fall for, trust or give credit to those who are sycophantic towards them. Rather, they trust and give credit to those who do good things for others and who do their jobs very well, even when these others are not directly in front of them.

Those who do their duties and jobs very well, regardless of whether or not others are around them, are not immediately recognized by others. But as time goes by, they are recognized, trusted and respected by many people.

When you try to cover someone else's eyes, it is just like you are covering your own eyes. But when you do your duty and job well, you are making yourself shine.

657. March 9, 1994. Paris

You promise yourself that you want to help others, that you want to make others happy and that you will not be negative. This promise is so strong that you even deliver it to yourself while you sleep: "I want to help others, I want to make others happy, and I do not want to be negative."

Because you promise it to yourself in your sleep, when you wake up in the morning your mind and body feel very light. But then the speech and action of the first person you meet in the morning disappoint you and make you feel lousy. So without even realizing it, you automatically become negative.

But in a corner of your mind your promise then appears: "I want to help others, I want to make others happy, and I do not want to be negative." With the appearance of that thought, you automatically say to yourself, "Forget it. Let me put my disappointment and negativity down." The very next moment, you automatically smile and say to that person, "Good morning! May I get you some coffee or tea?"

658. March 10, 1994. Paris

When you are angry at others, dislike and blame others, you put yourself far away from the realm of Buddha and separate yourself from many people.

The reason many people get angry at others and dislike and blame them is that they do not know their true self. But even without clearly knowing it, they do realize that their true I comes from the realm of Buddha. That is why, when someone makes Buddha and bodhisattva actions, others follow, like and respect that person. And it is why, when someone makes sentient beings' action, others do not follow, like or respect that person.

When you always make good actions, you become a Buddha and bodhisattva; but when you always make bad actions, you become a sentient being. So according to your actions, you either become a Buddha or a sentient being.

But behind the Buddhas and sentient beings, there is a no-Buddha; and that no-Buddha's round face is always full with love and compassion, shining roundly.

P. S. *This is an enlightenment teaching. Carefully read and realize the last sentence.*

659. March 11, 1994. Munich

As your practice continues, your karma is eliminated and your body and mind begin feeling very light. But whenever karma is eliminated, the ego becomes bigger and you easily become confused about whether your karma is being eliminated or whether it is becoming bigger.

Ego comes from karma I. So as karma disappears, the ego wants to protect itself; that is why it becomes much bigger than before. But if while eliminating your karma you make bodhisattva karma, then that ego becomes a bodhisattva; and the more your karma disappears, the more that bodhisattva does great bodhisattva action. You then make everyone happy and are respected very much by others. Without showing off or protecting yourself, you always appear to be higher than others, are needed by others, and receive great love from all the Buddhas.

660. March 12, 1994. Munich

In the bright and clear realm of Buddha, a Buddha is made into a bodhisattva, and that bodhisattva gives birth to a Buddha. That baby Buddha becomes a bodhisattva, and that bodhisattva again becomes a Buddha and makes all sentient beings into bodhisattvas. All of those bodhisattvas then accomplish Buddhahood.

All Buddhas again become Buddhas. But why do those Buddhas only go for the eyes, ears, nose, tongue, body and mind? Why? Do not only have an interest and take pleasure in those six friends. If your interest changes into interest in the non-interesting Buddha, you then become a Buddha again and will make those six interesting friends into bodhisattvas. Those bodhisattvas then make delicious cakes out of karma, which they then feed to others and to themselves, and whoever eats those cakes again becomes a Buddha.

661. March 13, 1994. Munich

Because those who lie regularly have a habit of lying, they do so without hindrance; and because they do not even realize they are lying, they think they are telling the truth. As time goes by, their lies always come out. They lose the respect of others, and no one wants to deal with them anymore.

But when people lie in front of an awakened person, the fact that they are lying appears immediately. Yet awakened people do not complain about or hate those who are lying; they accept others' lies knowingly and do not scold or hurt them. Instead, awakened people give those who lie more love, deal with them truthfully, and make them more comfortable than others. In their previous lives, those who lie now did not receive true love or care.

Clear people do not discriminate between lying and telling the truth, but go beyond lying and telling the truth, always showing those who lie the clear path until they realize the truth and do not lie anymore.

662. March 14, 1994. Paris

It is easy to compliment and make others happy. But when others make a mistake it is difficult to bring it out and show them their mistake directly. It is especially difficult to point out directly the mistakes of those who have a lot of ego and greed, and show them their own ego and greediness.

When you point out others' mistakes to them, you must be very clear. If those who are clear make someone else feel bad by pointing out his or her mistake, even if only for a second, it brings them a lot of suffering. Clear people know others' suffering as their own, and so when they point out others' mistakes to them and teach them truly, they always take on the others' suffering and have difficulty sleeping for many nights. This is a bodhisattva's great sadness and suffering. But when everyone else becomes a bodhisattva and a Buddha, then this bodhisattva's suffering disappears.

Do many nice things while you are healthy because when you are sick, you cannot.

663. March 15, 1994. Paris

Sometimes people wonder where their life-destiny comes from. Our life-destinies are not determined by someone else; it is what we make ourselves.

If you practiced in your last life, were clear and did many nice things for others, then in this life you are respected by others and everything goes very smoothly for you. And if you practice in this life, do many nice things for others and do not dirty this realm of Buddha, but make it clear, bright and beautiful, then in your future during this life and in your next life you will continuously do good things for others, will be respected by others, and will live happily.

But even if you practice in this life and do many good things for others, it may sometimes seem that things do not go smoothly and are blocked. At that kind of time, continue to practice hard and things will become unblocked and will run smoothly. When that happens, it is just as though Buddha or someone came and helped you. At that time, appreciate that Buddha who helped you, appreciate the practice, and appreciate your master who shows you the path of practice.

That mind of appreciation will protect you and will lead you to the path of happiness. It is that mind of appreciation which will give you your life destiny.

664. March 16, 1994. Paris

When the eyes of a Buddha look at this whole world, it is infinitely beautiful. But when the eyes of a sentient being look at this whole world, it is difficult and full of suffering.

When you look at this world with Buddha eyes, your thinking, speech and action become beautiful, and you do not want to make others suffer. Even if someone hurts you or makes you suffer, you help and protect that person with love and compassion. And because you do not want that person to make others suffer, you practice and work for him until he attains Buddha eyes. Then, when he attains Buddha eyes, you forget about him.

A practice person's suffering does not last for long and his happiness is infinite. The person who knows what happiness is and is happy himself makes everyone beautiful.

665. March 17, 1994. Paris

If you really want to help others, always offer what you have yourself. If you say that you want to help others, but rather than offering what you have, you offer what others have, that is not helping. That is just an idea which takes away your credit and shows how stingy and greedy you are.

There is an old saying: "The person who has one hundred tons of beans, but who always looks to get a pound of someone else's beans, loses his or her one hundred tons of beans. But those who have only a single bean and yet cut it in half to share with someone else gain one hundred tons of beans."

The true path of offering means offering from what you have yourself; whether that is small or large does not matter. When you offer in this way, others will follow you and will accept your suggestions.

666. March 18, 1994. Rhein Ruhr

When your mind is clear and you take up a pen to write, the meaning of what you write is clear. But when you have a lot of delusion and you write, the meaning of what you write is not clear.

Human life is similar to that: when one's mind is clean, one's life is simple and comfortable, and one's simple and comfortable life becomes an example for others. But when one has a lot of delusion, one's life is complicated, one suffers a lot, and one confuses others.

In the clean mind you don't know how good you are, and because you feel that you are not good enough, you always try harder in order to fill in what is not good enough. But in the deluded mind, one always wants to show off and be better than others.

Fill your pen with love ink and compose your writing with compassionate meaning. Then your writing will be beautiful, and whoever reads it will become clean and comfortable.

667. March 19, 1994. Rhein Ruhr

No matter where you go, every place is your house; and no matter who you meet, everyone is your family.

If you think this way, you will never be a stranger or separate yourself from others; you will always be together with them. Also, the mind which misses your own house disappears, and you can put that missing mind into the present moment and completely devote yourself to it. When you can devote yourself to the present moment, you can make yourself comfortable and satisfied. That comfortable mind does not worry about the future and does not get caught by the past; you can use the present moment beautifully.

At that time, lazy mind disappears and that mind which is not lazy gives water to the shriveled flower in the vase before you, thus reviving the flower.

But if you insist on having a missing mind, always miss Buddha (absolute, truth). In that moment when you miss Buddha, you can discover your own Buddha and have infinite happiness.

668. March 20, 1994. Rhein Ruhr

A person who is good with numbers and figures seems to be very correct. But if that person gets caught by numbers and figures, he or she is just like a very smoothly cut stone upon which the birds and butterflies cannot land and rest. So that stone is cold and lonely.

By contrast, clear people who are good with numbers and figures know what a tip is, and so when they make a calculation they always give a little extra to others, making them happy. The amount they give to others, however small or large, always brings a great benefit for them in the future.

When at first you do not want to give a single bean to others, but then you turn your mind around and give one to them, that one bean makes ten thousand baby beans, which come home to you.

The connection made by buying someone else a cup of coffee makes many great relationships for yourself in the future, and you will live happily.

669. March 21, 1994. Paris

A long time ago, there was a master who practiced by himself. While practicing one day in the quiet tranquility, he heard words spoken to him by a shining light and he realized many things. The speech that came out from the light was not that of a person or other entity.

This kind of occurrence marks the reappearance of teachings and realizations which you had in previous lives. Whatever correct actions, speech, and thoughts you made in lives long ago reappear when you are in tranquility, and then those correct actions, speech and thoughts become wisdom for you in the present life. When you are in the quiet tranquility, this wisdom shines on you, just like a light, and reawakens you.

But your incorrect actions, speech, and thoughts from previous lives make ignorance and bring suffering in the present life. When you are not quiet and tranquil, that ignorance envelops you and makes you still more ignorant. So always practice, put yourself into the quiet tranquility, discover your true I, and live day to day and moment to moment wisely.

P. S. This is a teaching for people who are attached to and caught by religion.

670. March 22, 1994. Paris

When you see a negative movie or television program that has a lot of suffering in it, forget about it as soon as possible. The reason is that negative stories with suffering in them always give you a bad feeling which affects your daily life and brings unnecessary suffering for you.

This is why Shakyamuni Buddha said that while practicing one should be selective about what one sees and hears and where one goes. If what you see and hear in the places you go is negative, try to avoid them, and also try to avoid interacting with negative people.

But when you become clear, no matter what you see and hear, and no matter where you go, you can change negativity into positivity. Then that positivity will lead you into unhindered tranquility and you will make everyone comfortable.

So until you become clear, be aware and cautious about what you see and hear and where you go.

671. March 23, 1994. Paris

Until the true I became Shakyamuni Buddha, Prince Siddhartha had many doubts and questions and much suffering for 29 years. Even though he lived such a luxurious life, all of his luxury did not make him happy. His luxurious life was a karmic effect which came from the good karma he had made in his previous lives.

But Prince Siddhartha was not satisfied with only having this good karmic effect. He had a glimpse that there is something very important behind karma, so he wanted to find that very important thing. With this intention, he did not fall headlong into his luxurious life, and with the aim of finding that important thing, he left home and did six years of ascetic practice.

After he found that true I which had been covered by karma, he realized that this true I was actually himself, who is Buddha; that is why he became Shakyamuni Buddha at the age of 35. Shakyamuni Buddha then taught for 49 years and finally went into nirvana.

Going into nirvana means that Shakyamuni Buddha took off his karmic clothes. In the true I, life after life, eternally, he changes his clothes and appears in this world; eliminating sentient beings' darkness, he teaches and leads them onto the path of Buddha.

Now, in this moment, where is Shakyamuni Buddha? Find Shakyamuni Buddha this Saturday, which is Buddha's Nirvana Day.

672. March 24, 1994. Bremen

When you help others, do you do so only for them, or do you do so for your own ego, desire, name or benefit? You should think about that. If you do it for your ego, desire, name or benefit, then when you help others, rather than being complimented by them, they complain about you.

If the person whom you want to help is already being helped by someone else, and then you appear and say that you want to help, that means that you are being disrespectful of the one who is already helping and that you want to show off, proving that you are better than others.

In order to truly help others, you must first be clear yourself. And in order to be clear, you must practice. Then, when others need you, you can help them 100 percent. But if someone does not need you, simply forget about him or her.

Even if you help others, never think that you are helping them; let go of that kind of thinking and have a thankful mind towards those you help, because without them you could not make the great karma which comes from helping others.

673. March 25, 1994. Bremen

When you have important things to do and your mind is worried about getting them done, all day long you have difficulty digesting your food and your circulation is not good. While doing those important things, you have worries and fears and want to stop, but instead you keep going on. Then at night, while sleeping, you have bad dreams and you cannot sleep comfortably. When you get up in the morning, you get up with a headache, and you feel as though you can barely move. But you get up anyway, do your job 100 percent, and you finally accomplish those important things.

The meaning of this is that you must take care of your important things yourself, and you should realize that not being able to digest your food and having bad dreams means that whatever you do, blockages always appear.

Practicing and attaining enlightenment are similar to this. While doing your practice, you often want to quit. But because you have patience and endurance, and you continuously practice, you eventually attain enlightenment. By attaining enlightenment, you become clear and healthy, and whatever suffering and difficulty you had before is transformed into great teaching material for others, and shows you how to help them correctly.

In clarity and tranquility there is good health. But worrying and being fearful create sicknesses. So bury all of your worries and fears in the mantra and leave everything up to your true I (absolute, Buddha, truth). Then you will automatically attain enlightenment.

674. March 26, 1994. Bremen

A wise horse only sees the shadow of the whip and runs.

An unwise horse does not run even if whipped.

When someone points to the moon, rather than seeing the moon, an unclear person only sees the pointing finger and falls into discriminations, saying things like: "that finger is short" or "that finger is long" or "that hand is fat" or "that hand is thin."

True I (absolute, Buddha, truth) is the jewel, and with that jewel you can do anything. When you find and realize true I, all of your suffering disappears and you can make yourself and others comfortable. This is beyond medicine. When you find that which is beyond medicine, you no longer make discriminations.

Find true I as soon a possible through practicing; attain that which is beyond medicine and make yourself and others healthy. Become a wise horse and place that which is beyond medicine on your horse back. Then everyone will be made healthy wherever this horse goes.

675. March 27, 1994. Bremen

Shakyamuni Buddha and all previous masters realized nothingness and understood its theory. They realized that everything comes from and returns to nothingness, and they realized its power and beauty. Because they also realized that nothingness is love and compassion, they saved all sentient beings. During each century, many masters have appeared, and they still do so in order to continuously save all sentient beings.

With the human body, which we call "something," it is difficult to realize and become one with nothing. But the moment someone becomes one with nothing, that "something" realizes the correct path of somethingness, and in that moment receives wisdom from nothing. This wisdom is not from something. Yet in that moment, this something is not getting caught by something (I, my, me, my condition); it shines upon others, protects and helps them.

When you get caught by something, everything becomes difficult. But when you realize nothingness, your something is eternally happy, and it gives infinite love and compassion to others.

676. March 28, 1994. Paris

When you are in difficulty and suffering, you want more help from Buddha (absolute, truth). At that time you repeat the mantra vigorously and you surprise yourself that, without thinking, you can vigorously go into the mantra, that when you strongly practice 100 percent you overcome your difficulty, and that the suffering which you had leads you to having realization.

That mind and action which does the mantra vigorously makes you forget your delusion, and the mantra then connects you with your truth, which was hiding behind your delusion. That I which connects with true I brings the power and wisdom to overcome difficulty. Then the difficulties and situations of suffering that you had been experiencing become great teachings for you, and if in the future you have the same situation again, you will not suffer from it; you will know how to handle it. That experience also becomes a great method to help and teach others.

677. March 29, 1994. Paris

Today, keep your mind comfortable.

The busier you are and the more things you have to do, the more you should keep your mind comfortable and tranquil. When you keep your mind comfortable and tranquil, no matter how many things you have to do, you do not get nervous, negative or tight; you can perform your duties correctly, one by one.

Do not try to finish all of your work at one time and do not expect the results to come immediately. Whatever work must be done now, do now; and whichever results you must wait for, wait for. See yourself and appreciate yourself for doing difficult things, and appreciate whoever gives you those difficult jobs. That mind of appreciation will make you comfortable and tranquil, and then you can enjoy your job and fulfill your duties correctly, one by one. If you enjoy your job, the results of your work will make others happy and they will respect you.

678. March 30, 1994. Honolulu

When you come to a place that has good nature energy, your ego can easily become bigger; you can easily become jealous of others, and you can easily pry into others' business. This means that a healthy person easily uses his energy for outside things, and that an unhealthy person easily uses his energy for inside things. Because a person who is not healthy is busy taking care of his unhealthy body and puts his energy into curing himself, he does not do things which hurt others. Also, that person promises himself, "When I become healthy I will do many good things for others."

There is an old oriental saying: "While in paradise one speaks too much, but while in hell one is quieter and practices to get out of hell quickly and go to paradise." This means that when you really wish for what you want, your strong wishing mind goes one step further. That mind has no you or I, and because that mind becomes very clean, without having any dust, it makes your wish come true.

When you are in a good place and you practice, you do not say unnecessary things and you work for others. Then you do not get caught by heaven or hell. Also, wherever you go you find the infinite, true I, and whether you are in a good or bad place, you do bodhisattva actions for others and live a truly happy life, eternally.

679. March 31, 1994. Honolulu

A long time ago, someone did straight hook fishing and quietly waited for his time to come. When that time came, he was successful.

This means that while going on your path, you must wait until your goal is accomplished. While waiting, do not make bad karma;

and while in the quietude, polish yourself. Whatever situation you have, and especially when you are planning big things, timing is very important. Until your time comes, prepare for the accomplishment of those important things and wait. The experience you have while waiting is more important than the experience you have when success comes. An impatient person always makes mistakes, but a person who knows how to wait has great success that others cannot follow.

Attaining enlightenment is similar to this. Practice, polish yourself, and wait patiently. Then, when the time is right, you will attain enlightenment.

680. April 1, 1994. Honolulu

You often promise yourself that you would like to be a bodhisattva. But while going on the bodhisattva path, you find that if someone irritates and angers you, you cannot coordinate your daily schedule and your life becomes confused. That makes going on the bodhisattva path more difficult for you and makes it hard to do bodhisattva actions.

This does not mean that going on the bodhisattva path is difficult or that doing bodhisattva action is difficult. It means that your own path is not yet deep. If you are clear and truly attain love and compassion, then even if someone irritates you or hurts your feelings, you are not caught by this. And if you realize true I, which is the original place of love and compassion, then even if someone confuses you and disrupts your daily schedule, you do not blame him. This is just like when you clean your room very neatly and then your child comes in and messes it up: you do not get angry at your child; you clean the room again and appreciate the fact that your child is with you.

Appreciate others who make you change your routine and who test your path. When you truly understand 100 percent what appreciation is, then no one can hinder or bother you. You can live a correct life and do true bodhisattva actions.

A correct life is a life of doing bodhisattva actions.

681. April 2, 1994. Honolulu

While practicing and making yourself bright and clear, once in a while old habits appear. For example, sometimes you meet an old friend or you go to a place you used to frequent, and without realizing it your old habits appear. Afterwards, you experience regret and dislike yourself because of the speech and actions you made during those times, and you tell yourself, "Why didn't I act and speak better than that?"

At those kinds of times, do not blame yourself and do not have regrets. Instead, be happy that now you can see your own speech and actions and appreciate the practice through which you can clearly see yourself. As time goes by, you will be able to fix your old habits, you will not make the same mistakes again, and you will also know how best to create your new self.

682. April 3, 1994. Honolulu

The person who is greedy for power gets hurt by power.
The person who is greedy for money gets hurt by money.
The person who is greedy for sex gets hurt by sex.

But;

If you are not greedy for power, but you are greedy to treat, help and protect everyone equally, then you automatically become a hero.

If you are not greedy for money, but you are greedy to satisfy and benefit everyone, then you automatically become rich.

If you are not greedy for sex, but you are greedy to use sex mind — which is the mind that wants to be close to others, to love and care for others — then you automatically become a Buddha and a bodhisattva.

683. April 4, 1994. Honolulu

Behind joking is always some truth. When you try to slight others by joking, you actually slight yourself and show your truth in an ignorant way.

But when wise people joke, they joke with a mind of respect, and so their jokes make whoever hears them happy.

Always be careful of what you let out of your mouth. And if someone makes a bad joke about you, do not become angry. Rather, treat that person compassionately and give him a beautiful joke in return to make him realize his mistake.

684. April 5, 1994. Honolulu

Love the people, but be careful of the people.

Be careful of the people, but also be careful of yourself.

Be careful of yourself, but see that mind which sees being careful.

When you can see that mind which sees being careful, and that mind is bright and clear, then, in the love which has no you or I, without being careful, you can care for and protect everyone.

685. April 6, 1994. Honolulu

When you try to be better than someone else, many obstacles always appear. The more you try to be better than someone else, the more that person tries to be better than you. The reason is that the mind which tries to be better than others is ego mind, and so you both are just fighting each other with your egos. That creates blaming mind and revenge mind.

If you really want to be better than others, first truly lower yourself and give yourself to others. Lowering yourself means breaking your own ego, and giving yourself to others means breaking others' egos. When you do this you will not have blockages or hindrances, and so the truth will appear between yourself and others. Then you will understand each other, you will know each other, and you will automatically protect one another. Without winning or losing, you will connect with and love one another.

686. April 7, 1994. Yun Hwa Dharma Sah

In the past, many masters put their bodies through a lot of suffering in order to find the beautiful truth which is beyond the body. They taught the truth to everyone, and with the truth they taught them how to keep their present form correctly and how to think, act and speak correctly. This means that they taught about the karma one makes through one's body, and how to prevent the karma one has made from negatively affecting one so that one can find infinite, true I and live eternally, without any distinctions.

But, if you always think about others, do not bother others and live for others, then without putting your body through suffering you can find true I and attain the truth.

Living for others is not easy. But if you do that which is not easy, true I makes correct thinking, action and speech, and then you can live an eternally appreciative and happy life.

687. April 8, 1994. Yun Hwa Dharma Sah

Love comes from the place of nothing. The whole universe is full with love.

If you know love only through feelings and you try to verify its existence only through feelings, then that means you do not yet know what love is. And if when you feel good, you love, and when you do not feel good, you do not love, then that means your love is only form and karmic love, not true love.

Those who attain love which is beyond form and karma know what true love is, can love others equally and receive love from others. They can attain true compassion which eliminates all the difficulties of sentient life and which extends beyond sentient life. People like this can have absolute love, and with that love they can create true beauty. Wherever they go, they can beautifully adorn that place.

This is the true bodhisattva life.

688. April 9, 1994. Honolulu

While listening to people speak, sometimes it seems that there is no point in what they are saying, that they explain everything in a long and roundabout way, and that there is negative energy in what they say.

When those whose practice path is deep listen to this kind of speech, they hear but do not listen, and afterward forget everything they heard. But when those whose practice path is not deep listen to that kind of speech, they become confused, and afterward their energy is negative. They then complain about the one who spoke and judge whether the point of what he or she said is right or wrong, thus making suffering for both themselves and the speaker.

Practice people, do not open your mouth before your point is clear, and when you speak, speak briefly and clearly so you do not waste the time and energy of whoever is listening to you. When you speak, speak with the truth, and speak in order to make others feel good and to lift them up. This is the bodhisattva's and leader's way of speech.

689. April 10, 1994. Honolulu

Even though you stay together with someone else, sometimes you are so comfortable together that you do not even notice that this person is there. And even though you become separated, you do not feel that you are really apart.

Whatever you think and do, always do so for one another and protect each other. When you act in this way, your relationship becomes infinite, you benefit one another, you make one another happy, and with that happiness you make everyone happy.

Are your relationships with others this kind of relationship or not? Try to see if this is so, and if not, strive to realize this kind of relationship with others.

Remember what our true I is — that true I which is never separate from others.

690. April 11, 1994. Honolulu

When you are in a negative situation, do not become nervous or frightened.

First, settle and calm your mind. The method to settle and calm your mind is to think about Buddha (absolute, truth) and repeat the mantra. Second, do not cast blame or complain about that negative situation which came to you. Instead, think about how you can handle the situation in a wise and stylish way. You will then surprise yourself with the wisdom that appears and allows you to handle the situation smoothly, without hurting others.

Then, when that situation is finished, do not think about it anymore and do not boast to others about how well you handled it. Forget the whole thing.

691. April 12, 1994. Honolulu

In the wide, empty space I lie down, widely open my arms and legs, and breathe. At that time, I become one with the empty space and the empty space becomes one with me; there are no hindrances. So why can I not get away from the spider web life? And why do I get caught by this and that?

If I put down that thinking which gets me caught, then that spider web is in the palm of my hand. It is just like knitting a sweater. If I knit each stitch correctly, one by one, it becomes a beautiful sweater. But if I miss even one stitch, it is ruined.

Do your work every day, without neglecting any part of it. And keep your mind like the wide, empty space.

692. April 13, 1994. Honolulu

Today, show your appreciation for nature — for the mountains, the oceans, the land and the sky — and wish for them to be comfortable and beautiful.

Because all of nature comes from true I (Buddha, absolute, truth), it is just like your own family, brothers and sisters. So if you wish for nature to be comfortable and beautiful, that is making yourself comfortable and beautiful.

Nature and we human beings are not separate. Realize that we are all connected. If you do so, you will know how to take care of nature.

693. April 14, 1994. Honolulu

The place of Buddha is soft, bright, clear and comfortable. That is why Buddha's face has a soft, beautiful and compassionate smile. That smile is to help all sentient beings.

The life of sentient beings is usually hard and difficult. But if you smile all of the time, no matter how hard a situation you have, you can change it into a soft situation and can overcome all difficulties.

When you are in difficulty and have obstacles, think about Buddha's soft and comfortable place and even try imitating his beautiful smile. Then that Buddha who is in front of your eyes will answer you with a smile.

Today, try to smile all day long, no matter what.

694. April 15, 1994. Honolulu

Think about the exquisite theory and function of the inside of the black point.

When you and the thing which sees the black point become one, you will realize the theory of being one with the universe. At that time, you will realize the emptiness of universal space. When you realize the emptiness of universal space, you will know how to utilize your time. When you know how to utilize your time without bothering others, you will realize the infinity of your time. When you realize the infinity of your time, you can eliminate your impatience, fears and insecurities. Then you will know how to use the exquisite power of the black point.

Remember, using the exquisite power is for everyone.

P. S. Meditate deeply upon this teaching.

695. April 16, 1994. Honolulu

Babies and children also have their own opinions and rights. So babies and children like people who follow their opinions and respect their rights, and dislike those who do not.

Do not disparage babies or children, and realize that they, too, are human beings. As you raise them, show and give your children full respect. Then, without scolding them you can teach them correctly and can raise them to be great human beings. They will appreciate and respect you, and there will be no walls or negativity in your relationships with one another. Then you and your children can be the closest friends in the world, and you can protect and make one another happy.

Do not blame your child if he does not listen to you, and do not blame your own parents if they do not listen to you. Instead, raise your own mind of respect.

P. S. Remember that in children's eyes, adults are stupid.

696. April 17, 1994. Honolulu

In human life, it always seems that behind happiness is sadness, behind health is sickness, and behind satisfaction is dissatisfaction. So it is difficult to be truly and eternally happy, healthy and satisfied. And even if you are happy, you really do not know what happiness is; even if you are healthy, you really do not know what health is; and even if you are satisfied, you really do not know what satisfaction is. So it is always difficult to get away from worries and agonies.

Even though we live this kind of life, those who seek the truth and dharma still truly believe that there is truth beyond the world of opposites. With that belief, they finally conquer the human world of opposites and finally realize and attain the truth.

But until you realize and attain the truth, there is a way to eliminate your present suffering. The way to do so and to go beyond the world of opposites is to make everyday life stylish and beautiful. In order to make everyday life stylish and beautiful, do not be lazy, strive to use your time very efficiently, and always think about how to live a stylish and beautiful life. Then the truth will always be with you and will protect you.

Striving in this way will make you realize and attain the truth in a short time. After realizing and attaining the truth, you will not be afraid of the world of opposites; and without leaving this world, you will illuminate with compassion and will benefit and make everyone happy.

The lotus flower that is wet with the early morning dew makes today more stylish and beautiful.

697. April 18, 1994. Honolulu

When I see Buddha's bright and clear place, I can see you.
When you see Buddha's bright and clear place, you can see me.
But when you attach to your six senses, which appear with your body and mind, you cannot see me; you get caught by the three poisons, and you cannot even see yourself. Then you blame me and say that I do not see, care for, or protect you. How sad that is.

Before you blame me and complain about me, eliminate the three poisons through doing the mantra, and leave behind attachment to the six senses through doing samadhi.

See Buddha's bright and clear place. How is it?
Do you see me?
Do you see yourself?
Now, how can you say that we are separate for even one second?
Today, please be happy and comfortable.

698. April 19, 1994. Honolulu

That thing which sees the place of Buddha and which sees your own body and mind makes your life and creates everything. So when that thing is not clear to you, you ruin yourself and you ruin others. But when that thing is clear to you, you benefit and make yourself happy, and at the same time you benefit others and make them happy.

We are always using that thing, but when we do not know that thing, that not-knowing creates ignorance.

When you want to know that thing:

1. See your own mistakes.
2. When you can see your mistakes, do not be sad, do not be depressed, and do not be guilty.
3. Be happy that you can see your mistakes.
4. With that happy mind, fix your mistakes.
5. While you fix your mistakes, that thing will gradually become bright and clear, you will know the secret of that thing, and you will know the exquisite use of that thing.
6. You will realize that the exquisite use of that thing is to make others happy.
7. When that thing makes others happy, then that thing will make you shine.
8. You will then realize that this thing which makes you shine always remains in the place of nothingness.
9. When you realize that, you will again become a Buddha and a bodhisattva.
10. Then you can live eternally, without extinction.

699. April 20, 1994. Honolulu

We human beings come here to have a clear, calm and compassionate mind like Buddha and to act as bodhisattvas. This is why we are here, and this is our correct job and purpose in being here. But because we do not realize this, we have difficulties.

But when you realize this and keep your mind like that of a Buddha and act as a bodhisattva, then you no longer have the suffering of a regular human being; your suffering and difficulty will be different. Through your suffering and difficulty, you will learn more about how to do bodhisattva action; so even though you have suffering and difficulty, your mind is always like that of a Buddha.

Through this teaching, please realize correctly what our duties and jobs are in this life. Then you will never suffer like a regular human being.

700. April 21, 1994. Honolulu

People are usually in two-way street situations and they do not know which way they should go — this way or that way? It is like this in relationships, too. People do not know whether they should choose this person or that person. Because of this indecision, people always have big dilemmas.

In order to choose the correct way or person, do not only pursue that which will benefit you the most in the present moment. Even if you do not receive an immediate benefit, go for that which you will most appreciate and be proud of in the long run, considering how you can be most useful. Then success will always follow you in the future.

Water becomes mountain; mountain becomes water. We are always changing; so do not only look for what will benefit you and make you comfortable in the present moment.

701. April 22, 1994. Honolulu

Those who are awakened always protect and help everybody. While others sleep, they remain awake and protect the whole world. But when some other people wake up, those who are awakened can rest. And when everyone wakes up, then they can go to sleep. If there is even just one person who has yet to wake up, awakened people do not go to sleep. This is Buddha's great duty and responsibility.

When you are lazy, you cannot see Buddha; the reason people cannot wake up is because they are lazy. But when you are diligent you can live and rest with Buddha.

It is difficult to receive a human form. So, while you have this form, wake up; use this form to become a Buddha. Then, even if you cannot sleep, you will not get tired, and you can enjoy an eternal truth-form, like a Buddha.

Are you awake today?

702. April 23, 1994. Honolulu

In the night sky, some stars seem to shine brightly, while others seem not to.

It is the same thing in this world: some people seem to be very bright, while some others seem to be dark. But brightness and darkness are not made by someone else; we each make ourselves bright or dark. When you know that, you can change your darkness into brightness, and with that brightness you can shine on others and make them bright, too.

When you are in darkness, do not just sit in it; strive to change it to brightness. Then you will become bright. All human beings are the same; the only difference is how much one strives to be bright or how much one struggles and suffers in the darkness.

Remember, beyond brightness and darkness is nothingness. That nothingness is always clear and makes brightness and darkness, according to what one wishes.

As you know, our truth is beyond brightness and darkness.

703. April 24, 1994. Honolulu

Put energy into one place and concentrate your attention there; then *yin* and *yang* energies become balanced in that place. This balanced energy then accomplishes things according to correct intentions.

Correct intentions are beyond the world of I, my and me, beyond attachments and discriminations, and beyond the world of opposites. If you have intentions of this kind and concentrate on what you want to do, you can overcome all obstacles and accomplish what you want.

Beyond the world of I, my and me, and the worlds of attachments and opposites, is the non-self world. The non-self world is the world of you and me existing, and the world of non-separation between you and me.

Have a non-self intention and concentrate on your work. Then you will accomplish what you must and will be successful in whatever you aim to do.

When Buddha (the absolute, the truth) created the universe, nature and all sentient beings, he used this method. If you realize and attain this method yourself, whether you are a scientist, a philosopher, a psychologist, a religious person or whatever, you can find answers for all your questions.

704. April 25, 1994. Honolulu

Today, forget everything.
Whatever thinking appears, let it disappear.
Then forget that which disappeared.
Try to forget everything; relax and let nature take care of everything.
Abide in great space.

705. April 26, 1994. Honolulu

Today is a day during which you must work very hard. Whatever unfinished jobs you have, try to finish them today. Move your body just like a horse and gallop. Today is a day to think less and to put things into action.

Do so from today and for the next week; move your body and act. If you do not have anything to do, go outside and even clean up someone else's garbage. The reason for this is that during this week, nature-energy is becoming lively. So the more you physically move your body, the more you can receive that lively nature-energy and have a healthy mind and body.

706. April 27, 1994. Honolulu

Even in a difficult situation, do not become disappointed; and when you are in a happy situation, do not lose yourself because of happiness.

From time to time, appreciate that you are in this world and that you can taste human life, each thing in itself, widely and deeply.

When there is high there is low, and when there is wide there is narrow. When you have realized this and you are high, you are not arrogant; when you are low, you do not become disappointed or depressed; when there is wideness, you do not become lazy; and when there is narrowness, you do not become impatient.

When you are like this, how can you be confused? Placing that self which is not confused into tranquility, it is possible to see true I emanating wisdom from time to time. That radiant wisdom always remains tranquil; without being hindered anywhere, it is ever shining

707. April 28, 1994. Las Vegas

Greed makes you ignorant and places you in darkness. There you cannot find yourself; you wander around suffering.

Even if you gain some benefit from being greedy, that benefit eventually will ruin you. But if you are not greedy, nobody can confuse, seduce or lead you into darkness.

Greed which is only for yourself makes you become a sentient being. But if you have great greed in order to make others happy, to benefit everybody, to adorn this Buddha land beautifully and rescue all sentient beings, then that great greed makes you become a Buddha and a bodhisattva.

708. April 29, 1994. Las Vegas

If people commit themselves to achieving a goal and they keep pursuing it without respite, even though they may experience setbacks along the way, they will achieve their goal. Their accomplishment will surprise everybody, and they will be fascinated by the result.

When people make a commitment with a mind which has no hindrance and does not shake, that commitment eliminates small I and becomes Big I, which means becoming connected with absolute energy. That is why if one's commitment is strong, the goal will always be reached.

If your goal is only for yourself, reaching it will only ruin you and others. But if your goal is for everyone's benefit, reaching it will bring benefit that will shine forever to you and to others .

709. April 30, 1994. Las Vegas

According to the system of *fong su* or knowledge of nature's energy (in Chinese: *fengshui*), there are places which let energy flow out and places which retain energy.

People have difficulties living comfortably in places which let energy flow out; things do not work out for them the way they would like, and so they eventually move away. But people live comfortably in places which retain energy. Those places attract people to come and stay, and in those places many interesting creations appear which tempt everyone.

When people in the Orient build a house, buy land or move from one place to another, they look for the kind of place which retains energy, just like a human being's *tan chun* (the point below the belly button). In places which let energy flow out, if peoples' minds are clean and they do many good things for others, their great intentions will serve to hold the energy and make those places attract many people. When people are like this, they create correct things for others and transform places which let energy out into places of infinite good luck.

710. May 1, 1994. Las Vegas

When you meet one good person, because of that person everything becomes smooth and comfortable. You can be very satisfied, and at the same time, because of that person, you become important.

But when you meet one wrong person, whatever virtue you have built up is diminished, and at the same time you lose yourself, your reputation, and you suffer.

Do not take any single person lightly. And when you deal with others, do not lose yourself. When you deal with negative people, strive not to become negative yourself; and when you deal with positive people, strive not to let your ego grow.

Whether you are with positive or negative people, treat whoever you deal with like a Buddha. Then you will not dirty or lose yourself; you will become a Buddha yourself.

711. May 2, 1994. Honolulu

The more you treat unwise people nicely, the larger their egos grow, the more they think that they are special, and the more they want to be better than the person who teaches and cares for them.

The more a wise person is respected by others, the humbler he or she becomes.

Being humble makes others happy. Having ego makes enemies of others. Humility creates a beautiful fragrance, and it makes others happy and comfortable. Ego becomes a thorn which keeps its possessor from being free.

712. May 3, 1994. Honolulu

Our human form exists in the place of nothingness.

Our human form is transient.

We do not know when we will be able to have a human form again.

While we have this human form, why do we have to become angry, show off, hurt others, blame others, take others' time and become cranky because we cannot get what we want?

There are times when people will say they do not like this or that situation, or this or that person. So they change their situations and find someone else. These changes at first seem preferable to what they had before, but soon the same problems appear and are sometimes even worse than before. This all brings more suffering and headaches.

If you realize even a little that this is human life, if you realize even a little that we live in the place of nothingness, if you realize even a little that our form is transient, and if you realize even a little that we do not know when we will receive a human form again, then you can escape your ignorance, you can live a little brighter life, and you can handle your human situations and relations a little more brightly.

713. May 4, 1994. Honolulu

People do not know what will be in the future.

Do not only judge others by their present situation. For example, just because people presently are poor and have nothing, do not disparage them; and just because people are presently rich and have many things, do not be sycophantic towards them. People's lives are always changing and turning like a wheel. So no matter who you deal with, treat everyone equally.

But when people act correctly, respect and compliment them; and when people act wrongly, give them a warm look without saying anything. Also, always encourage young people and always make old people comfortable.

The difficulty which you have in your young days becomes medicine later on. So young people: do not think of your present difficulties as suffering. Think of everything as adding to your stock of experience, and when you have difficulty do not fall down. Of course, if you do fall down a little bit, get up, dust off your hands and knees, and continue on your path. Then success will be right in front of your eyes.

714. May 5, 1994. Honolulu

When love is big, hate is big.

When there is no love, there is no hate.

It is difficult to love the person you hate. But when hate is gone, non-love love appears. Non-love love does not have hate or love. That love loves infinitely.

When you realize what this means, you can have true love, which is non-interested love. Then you will never be hindered or get dirtied by anyone, and you can just love.

This is simple but powerful love.

715. May 6, 1994. Honolulu

Shakyamuni Buddha's teaching is: "Believe and follow my teachings (dharma), but do not believe or follow me. And while believing and following my teachings, believe your mind which believes and follows my teachings." That is right!

If your mind does not believe and follow the teachings, nobody can save you. This is a special sentence. Your mind makes you a Buddha and a bodhisattva, your mind makes you a sentient being, and your mind makes you happy or unhappy.

When you clean your mind and become one with Buddha's clear mind, at that time there is nothing to believe or follow; you are already one with Buddha's mind, and that one mind has already saved yourself and others.

But until that time, believing and following the teachings insures that you are being saved. If you do not yet believe and follow the teachings, you must practice harder to be able to do so.

P. S. With this teaching you can distinguish between realization and religion. Buddhism is realization.

716. May 7, 1994. Los Angeles

You live in Buddha. But due to your desire, anger, ignorance and five desires, you are not able to be near Buddha. In order to draw near to Buddha, first eliminate the three poisons and five desires. Then you can begin going near Buddha.

When you are in the three poisons and five desires, you see Buddha through your imagination. Upon eliminating the three poisons and five desires, you will see Buddha as you never even imagined. Then, going near Buddha, you deal with Buddha without hindrance.

When you can see Buddha without hindrance, that non-hindered mind is already Buddha, and that non-hindered Buddha always uses energy to make others into beautiful Buddhas and bodhisattvas. At that time, the three poisons and five desires become eight methods for accomplishing this, like a woven lotus flower; and wherever that lotus flowers goes, it fills that place with a beautiful fragrance.

717. May 9, 1994. Paris

Because you feel like doing something but don't know what to do, it seems that you are always wasting your time. And, because you are not satisfied with your present life situation, you become cranky.

But at those times do not become cranky; and just because you are not satisfied with your life, do not bother others, and do not let your crankiness spill over onto them.

Your habits and ways of doing things are your karma. Fixing them thus means fixing your karma and eliminating your blockages. As you fix your habits and ways of doing things, new wisdom appears and that new wisdom shines on you. Then you find new methods of living life that you never expected. Those new methods make you excited and give you new appreciation of life with which you can really make life very interesting and satisfying.

718. May 10, 1994. Paris

People like to see and judge others according to their own point of view. When, according to their point of view, they see things that 'are' wrong, they say that they are bad; and when, according to their point of view, they see things that 'are' correct, they say that they are good. But if instead of seeing your own point of view subjectively, you see it objectively, you can see that your own point of view has many faults.

Do not be obstinate about your own point of view. If it is not accepted or respected by others, do not continue to insist that you are correct. If you can see your own point of view objectively, your obstinacy, ego and troubles with others will disappear. Then your own point of view will become everyone's point of view, and it will help everyone go in the correct direction and have faith in and respect for one another.

719. May 11, 1994. Paris

When sentient beings are angry at others, they try to get back at one another in a bad way. But when Buddhas see bad situations, they always deal with others in a good way.

When people hurt, bother or irritate you, do not deal with them angrily. Instead, deal with them quiescently and with good actions.

Those who bother and hurt others do so because they are insecure and do not have good karma. By dealing with such people quiescently and with good actions, you help them to become secure and to plant the seeds of good karma. Planting the seeds of good karma saves them, after which they will be able to save others.

Planting the seeds of good karma eliminates peoples' seeds of bad karma so that they become secure and do not hurt themselves or others.

720. May 12, 1994. Paris

Our original place is clean and full of goodness; that is where we come from. But as soon as we receive our human form, we can easily forget about this clean, goodness-filled place, and we can go into an unclear direction full of negativity. That makes us suffer.

Doing good things for others makes you happy and clear. But treating others negatively and bothering them leads to you also being bothered and suffering as well.

Thinking about Buddha (truth, absolute) leads you to your original, clean and goodness-filled place, and it helps you sustain presence there. So at the end of each day, make a habit of thinking about Buddha and of reviewing what you did that day. If you made any mistakes, try not to make them again; and if you did good things, forget about them because whatever good you do is just doing your correct human job.

721. May 13, 1994. Paris

If others hurt you, make you suffer, disparage you or are doing better than you, do not blame them or become angry or jealous. If you have the mind not to blame or become angry or jealous, and you have endurance and compassion, you are already a Buddha and a bodhisattva. That is not easy to do. But if you accomplish this, you are already teaching others. Then, by your actions you will help others to eliminate their bad seeds so they will not make others suffer.

If you practice for people who make others suffer, you are doing your great bodhisattva job. But your bodhisattva job is not actually a job; it is your duty and mission in this life.

If you do not have any doubts about your practice, you will never get caught by any negativity; you will be forever free.

722. May 14, 1994. Paris

We know that our path is to save all sentient beings. But before we can save all sentient beings, it is necessary to save ourselves, and even that is difficult. The reason is that people are busy satisfying their desires, attachments and greed. If they do not satisfy them, they become dissatisfied, cranky and angry; and if someone else is doing better than they are, they then become jealous.

But even if we have this kind of situation, knowing that we must save all sentient beings means that we all come from the place of Buddha, and that when we were there we all took a vow that on arriving in this *saha* world, we would save all sentient beings.

We have the form of a sentient being which easily has desires, greed and attachments, and which becomes jealous. But when we eliminate the problems which come from our form, we realize the place of Buddha, and we are able to keep the vows we previously took. Then we can perform our correct duties as human beings and will continuously, eternally, do our correct bodhisattva job and keep Buddha's mind.

723. May 15, 1994. Paris

Shakyamuni Buddha came into this world to shine light into sentient beings' dark minds and to teach us that although sentient beings' minds are covered by dark ignorance, behind that ignorance there is brightness and clarity: our original mind.

If it were not for Shakyamuni Buddha, in our ignorance we sentient beings would make nothing but bad karma; we would not be able to find our truth; we would always suffer in darkness; and it would be difficult to be rescued. Shakyamuni Buddha's realizations, wisdom and dharma always lead us onto the correct path and enable us to become Buddhas ourselves. Therefore, we should always appreciate him.

His birthday is the day we find light in darkness. It is precisely the mind of wishing him happy birthday that finds light in darkness. So let us sincerely wish Shakyamuni Buddha a happy birthday and repeat together:

"Happy Birthday to you dear Shakyamuni Buddha!"

Happy birthday to you all! Today is everyone's birthday.

724. May 16, 1994. Paris

When you can receive the respect and love of the person with whom you are closest, it is just like receiving the respect and love of everyone. But when you cannot harmonize with those with whom you are closest, you cannot harmonize with anyone else.

Helping others must start with those with whom you are closest. If you can help them, you can help others.

Today, begin helping others by helping the person with whom you are closest — whether that is a family member or friend, or someone else.

725. May 17, 1994. Paris

Today, let us get out from our ignorance, and, before we complain about others, let us see ourselves.

Life in this *saha* world seems to be long but it is not; it is very short. Time flows quickly, just like water: we are born into this world, we get old, and then we leave. So while you are here, do many good things and help others. Then, with that virtue you will always be reborn in a good place and you will live a happy and prosperous life, life after life.

Even though people say they want to help others, because of their own conditions, desire and greed, they often hurt others instead. And sometimes when people are on the correct path, someone else bothers them and they cannot comfortably proceed. How ignorant that is.

But there are some people who lay aside and cut off all of their conditions, desire and greed, and who, in order to save all sentient beings, want to attain enlightenment. So they go onto the great path, shave their heads and become monks and nuns. Reflect upon that at least one time.

Looking at it from some outsiders' points of view, the meaning of monks' and nuns' shaven heads seems to be that they are renouncing and rejecting the world because they cannot live a social life. But if people think that way it is a complete misunderstanding; they are seeing from an ignorant point of view.

Such courage! Because of the courage to lay everything aside and shave their heads, we should bow our heads down to monks and nuns, offering them great respect. That great courage eliminates all of their wanting, conditions, desire and greed; they cast them off like old shoes. Such courage! A regular human being does not have that kind of courage.

Sometimes a person who has a better situation than others complains all the time that he or she is not satisfied and continuously tries to satisfy his or her desires and greed. But if these people would understand even a little the great courage of monks and nuns, they would be able to see themselves and how they get caught by their own desires, greed and conditions, all of which throw them into suffering.

In our short human life, if we can sacrifice ourselves without putting our conditions, desire and greed into it, our minds of sacrifice will make us and others happy. Having a mind of sacrifice is the fast way to find our true self, and that beautiful mind is the mind which all human beings must have.

726. May 18, 1994. Paris

Eastern customs or Western customs are not the point. Wise people talk and debate less and show their intentions through their actions. Your mouth is to eat food and speak, but when you open your mouth too often, you scatter your energy; doing so, your head becomes unclear.

That is why people who talk a lot (with the exception of a translator or anyone whose job requires him to speak a lot) are unclear. But when you do not open your mouth too much, your head becomes clear and your eyes become bright; you can see everything very clearly. Then, with a clear head and bright eyes, when you open your mouth, you speak correctly. That correct speech does not hurt others; it helps them to realize themselves and makes them happy.

A single incorrect sentence is like a poison arrow which pierces both you and others. The creation of bad karma begins with the mouth. That is why the first sentence of the *Ten-Thousand Hands and Eyes Sutra* is, "*Jong gu op jin on, su ri su ri ma ha su ri, su su ri, sa ba ha*," which means, "Before I chant, I want to eliminate the karma that I created through my mouth."

The purpose of having discussions with others is to bring out correct ideas and to go in the correct direction. So during times of discussion, we need to open our mouths and speak. But we should not let unnecessary, personal feelings out of our mouths. Because our personal feelings change all of the time, just like the weather, if we express them too much, we cause the energy of those who are listening to go up and down. This is tiring for everyone and as a result no one does their job correctly.

There is an old saying: "Buddha's closed mouth is full with a smile, but sentient beings' open mouths are full with complaints. A wise person's single sentence can pay off a $100,000 debt, but an unwise person's 100,000 words cannot pay off even a one penny of his or her debt."

Secure people speak a little bit; insecure people speak a lot.

727. May 19, 1994. Paris

If you are unhappy, or if you think that you are unhappy, take the opportunity to reflect once again upon the perceptions you have of your life. Consider your daily habits. Maybe there is an important reason why you are unhappy.

See yourself a few times each day, especially while repeating the mantra. When you see yourself while repeating the mantra, it is just like seeing yourself in a clear mirror; you can see yourself very clearly. At such times, if seeing yourself brings up feelings of shame, do not indulge those feelings. Instead, fix what is wrong. And if seeing yourself brings up pride, guard against becoming arrogant.

When you are neither shameful nor arrogant, unhappiness cannot follow you and happiness will never make you ignorant.

728. May 20, 1994. Bologna

While practicing, if you stop, it does not feel good. Often, a negative situation will appear. But when you resume practicing, your problems disappear. Prior to practicing, you did not realize this; but once you have begun practicing, you are increasingly aware of this.

Sometimes you are assailed by doubts. "Did I make a mistake to start practicing? Did I get caught by practice? Am I too dependent upon practice?" The part of you that thinks it was a mistake to start practicing has its roots in laziness; the part of you that thinks that you got caught by practice is the part of you that cannot be free because it is already caught by many other things; and the part of you that thinks that you are too dependent upon practice has its roots in insecurity.

But when you practice diligently without conditions or doubts, all of your difficulties disappear, your path becomes bright, and you can see yourself. Then, without getting caught by anything, you rely on practicing and free yourself. That self which becomes free realizes how important, powerful and big practice is, and appreciates practice and whoever gave you the practice. Then you can always practice without conditions, and you thoroughly realize that practicing is the most important thing to do in this world.

729. May 21, 1994. Bologna

If you have Buddha eyes that see this world, human beings and all other things with love and compassion, there is nothing to get caught by, nothing to be angry about, nothing to be jealous of, and nothing for which to blame others. Then, there is only a great greed and desire to benefit and give contentment and happiness to all sentient beings. How beautiful that is!

Because we want to have Buddha eyes, we practice. But many times each day, we get caught by small I; we become angry, jealous and blame others. So how can we have Buddha eyes?

If you really want to have Buddha eyes, while going on the path you have to have patience and endurance. That patience and endurance will automatically enable you to attain Buddha eyes.

So even today, please be patient, have endurance, and practice in order to attain Buddha eyes so that you can see and truly attain the beauty of this whole world.

730. May 22, 1994. Bologna

Because I had a very good samadhi practice last night, I went to bed with a good feeling and a comfortable mind. But when I woke up this morning, without knowing why, I was cranky. I tried to let go of my crankiness, but I could not.

Feeling that way, instead of having a smile for the first person I met, I had a frown and a hard expression on my face. The sound of his saying "good morning" to me was very disagreeable. He smiled at me, but I did not like seeing his smile and I thought to myself, "What are you so happy about and why are you smiling?" His smiling face looked so ugly to me. Then, as he noticed my hard face, he also became hard and went away. I did not like that he looked at me even once.

For no reason at all, I felt badly all day and I did not want to do anything but cover myself in blankets and sleep all day long.

The point of the above story is that crankiness is the opposite of feeling good. According to East Asian correlative cosmology, because our bodies comprise *yin* and *yang* energies, when there is a good feeling, there is a bad feeling; and when there is a bad feeling, there is a good feeling. This theory explains the pattern of what appears from our human bodies and minds. So when you follow the feelings and emotions that appear from your body and human mind, you will find that there is no end to them, and that through following them you make nothing but unnecessary karma, putting yourself into a dark cloud and making yourself suffer.

As a practice people, when you have a bad feeling, do not become bad; and when you have a good feeling, do not be so happy about it. You must stay in the position from which you can see your own feelings rather than being swallowed up by them, and act from there. Then, when you have a bad feeling, you find it interesting; and when you have a good feeling, you find that interesting, too. If you do not get caught by either good or bad feelings, you are master of your own life.

Remember, life is interesting, and being happy or unhappy is all according to what you yourself make.

731. May 23, 1994. Paris

Today:
1) Do not bother others.
2) Do not make yourself suffer in delusions.
3) Give one inch to others.
4) Do not expect others to treat you well.
5) Think about how to make the person you are closest with happy, if even just for one moment.

Life is coming empty-handed, going empty-handed. So while you are in this world, cultivate skill in making others happy. Then you will receive a good harvest this life and next life too.

732. May 24, 1994. Paris

Give one more piece of cake to the person to whom you do not want to give anything, and spend one day with the person whom you do not want to see.

It is difficult to do what you do not want to do, but when you do so, your blockages open and your space, which was obstructed before, opens, too. You discover space that you did not even know about before.

When you accomplish this, it is not that you do not make cause and effect, but you no longer get caught by cause and effect. In our life we make cause and effect everyday; as long as our form exists, we cannot escape from it. But in order not to get caught by cause and effect, you have to know how to open yourself and eliminate your blockages. When you can open yourself and eliminate your blockages, your true self is right there, unhindered by like or dislike, and you see everything through great love and compassion eyes.

This is the way to live this present life freely, lovingly and beautifully.

733. May 25, 1994. Paris

What is the most joyful and happy moment of your day?

When you meet your lover?

When you receive money?

When you are noticed by others?

When you eat delicious food?

When you sleep very soundly?

When you have all these things, you are happy. But to the degree that you are happy about them, you must be responsible for them afterwards. So at first you are happy, but then worries appear, and those things no longer give you a clear and comfortable feeling.

Fortunately, there are moments when you can be fully happy and satisfied without having to be responsible and without worrying. Those are the moments when:

1) you make others happy,
2) you can help others,
3) others are happy.

These are the most joyful and happy moments of one's day, and they have no side effects.

734. May 26, 1994. Paris

There is an old saying, "When you are young you buy suffering. If you did not suffer when you were young, you will regret it when you become old." In other words, suffering is our teacher and those who never suffer cannot understand others and have difficulty helping them.

The striving and patience you have in wanting to conquer your suffering make you become a teacher and someone who is able to help and teach others correctly. Therefore, your suffering is not only for yourself; it is also for others. So do not think of your present difficulty as suffering; if you think of it as being for everyone, your suffering mind disappears and you can do your work 100 percent. The action of doing your work 100 percent helps you to get out of your suffering and also helps others to get out of their suffering.

735. May 27, 1994. Paris

When you find the end of a tangled thread and pull it, the whole thread straightens. But when you cannot find the end, the whole thread remains tangled and messy.

Finding that one end of the tangled thread is just like attaining enlightenment and realization. When you attain enlightenment and realization, all of your difficulties unexpectedly become easy and the process of resolving them one by one becomes very interesting. So intense is this interest that you would not trade it for anything. At that time, you also really appreciate life.

Attaining enlightenment and realization is the most important thing that we can do in this world. We do not eat and stay alive just to exist; we eat and stay alive in order to attain enlightenment and realization. That is why we practice.

Once you attain enlightenment and realization, you are free, life after life. So each day, do not waste your energy on small things; always practice and live to attain enlightenment and realization. If you really have a strong wish to attain enlightenment and realization, that mind will lead you to attain them.

So today let us eat, work and practice to attain enlightenment and realization.

736. May 28, 1994. Paris

Today we should all think about our parents, whether they are alive or they have passed away. When they brought us into this world, they had to bear great pain. Then they changed our diapers, gave us milk and raised us. Our parents always worry about us getting sick or hurt, and they are always wishing for us to become great. So we must have gratitude for their graciousness. We owe a lot to our parents, but it is a pity that often we cannot pay even 10 percent of the debt we owe them. Do not calculate what kind of parents you have or had; no matter how they are or were, you owe a lot to them.

If you meet wise parents, that is because of your good karma; and if you meet unwise parents, that is because of your negative karma. But no matter what, there are no bad parents. All parents love and live for their children. So we should greatly appreciate our parents.

If your parents have passed away, think about them today while repeating the mantra. And if your parents are alive, call them today and express your appreciation to them.

There is a true story about a 100-year-old mother who always worries about her 80-year-old daughter; she worries that she may become sick and that she may not eat well. Also, even today my own mother always worries about me — about how I dress, if I am eating well, and if I am okay or not.

So today, eliminate all blockages between you and your parents and just be thankful to them. Then you will feel great.

737. May 29, 1994. Paris

In this world there is endless fighting and competition to earn and have things. When you earn and have things, you are happy; and when you do not, you are sad. We live in endless suffering and then we pass away. Fighting and competing to earn and have things is very scary, whether it takes place at home or out in your social life.

A practice person should come out from fighting and competing to earn and have things. In order to do that, when you have a fight or are in a competitive situation with someone else, forget about what you want and let the other person have what he or she wants. In that moment, when you let others have what they want, it seems as though you failed and are stupid. But that is not true.

Let others have what they want, but then take care of your duties and do your work better and more sincerely than you did before. Then, as time goes by, without fighting or competing, whatever you want to have will come to you automatically, and it will make both you and others happy.

That wide, spacious mind which lets others have what they want has the power in it to earn everything.

738. May 30, 1994. Paris

The path of the practice life is just like going from a narrow path onto a wide one.

While going on the wide path you realize what that path means.

When you realize what that path means, as you are going along on it, the path disappears.

Then, while going along the path of no path, wherever you go you make a path.

While going on that path, beautiful colors, sounds, smells, tastes and touches go with you.

Those beautiful colors, sounds, smells, tastes and touches make both you and others happy, and that path which you made shines upon everyone.

739. May 31, 1994. Paris

Today's energy is very negative. So today watch your step, watch your mouth; do not become angry for no reason at all, do not make any important decisions, and smile more.

Tomorrow will be better.

740. June 1, 1994. Paris

When you find and become one with your true I, you never separate yourself from others. Then, even though you know everything clearly, you always discuss things with others and respect their opinions, and only then act. This is the way to avoid your ego and eliminate it without being in conflict with it.

Also, even though you become a Buddha and know everything, you should always depend upon Buddha and the dharma, and you should live with Buddha all of the time. Then you can do Buddha's correct function and duty.

What you know is what you do not know, and what you do not know is what you know. When you do not get caught by what you know and what you do not know, then you can help others correctly.

741. June 2, 1994. International Retreat, Munich

Your path had not been comfortable until one morning you met your true I and became one with it. One by one, the difficult things that were making your path uncomfortable become your teachers; one by one, those things become living lessons that teach you again and also teach others how to realize themselves.

That self which becomes one with the truth does not worry or think about the future. That self thinks of each day as being its whole life and gives itself entirely to the present. Because that self wants to do many good things for others, it puts all of its energy into benefiting and satisfying others, and it only thinks about how to make others happy.

When nighttime comes, that self sees itself and checks to see if it made any mistakes during the day, questioning whether it hurt or made others uncomfortable. If it did, this self vows that tomorrow it will not do so again. But if it benefited and made others happy and satisfied, it does not think about it anymore; it just goes to sleep.

742. June 3, 1994. International Retreat, Munich

When you get up in the morning, make that day's program.
1) See what work you must do today and what work you must do tomorrow.
2) What work you must do today, do today; and what work you must do tomorrow, leave for tomorrow.
3) Do not be fearful if you have a lot of work to do today.
4) Do your work today, but do it with a relaxed mind.
5) Do not check whether your job is a good job or a bad job.
6) Always appreciate the job which is given to you.
7) Respect whoever you meet today (whether you like or dislike that person) as a Buddha.
8) But when your body is sick, your duty is to relax 100 percent.

These are the ways to get a happy, healthy, wealthy and successful life. Remember, the present day is very important to your life.

743. June 4, 1994. International Retreat, Munich

A long time ago, Bodhidharma and the king had a conversation one day in which the king boasted that he did many good things for others and built many temples. So he asked Bodhidharma, "I did all of these things, so what kind of merit did I earn?" Bodhidharma replied, "*Mu* merit", which means nothing merit. The king did not understand Bodhidharma's answer, so he became angry and kicked him out of the palace.

When Bodhidharma said "*Mu* merit," it sounds as though he meant 'no merit,' but when you transcend the words, "*Mu* merit" does not mean 'no merit.' We must understand that in *Mu* (nothingness), everything is complete.

Not having is the essence of having, and having is the essence of not having. When you transcend having and not having, in not having there is everything. This 'not having' which is 'having everything' is our true I.

When you attain and become one with your true I, the three poisons (desire, anger and ignorance) and the five desires (for food, fame, sex, sleep and money) become your friends; the eight sufferings (being born, becoming old, getting sick, dying, not getting what you want, being separated from those you love, being with those you dislike and the imbalance of the five *skandas*) become your lovers; and out of the Four Noble Truths (suffering, the cause of suffering, the end of suffering and enlightenment) you build a long wall of love. Inside that long wall of love, everyone builds a house out of happiness. Everywhere inside the wall is permeated by a beautiful Dharma fragrance. And everywhere both inside and outside the wall, that fragrance brings compassionate smiles from the entire universe.

P. S. This is a very important teaching which has in it the essence of all the 84,000 sutras. Attain it!

744. June 5, 1994. International Retreat, Munich

This morning was beautiful and bright, but as soon as I got up I became caught by all kinds of delusions and forgot to make today's schedule. Instead, being in the delusions I felt good, then bad, then sad and then angry.

But suddenly I remembered the teaching that today is very important and that I should live entirely for today. Remembering that helped me to get out of the delusions, and then I was able to make today's schedule and put all of my energy into my work.

When I did so, my head suddenly became very light. And when I reflected on it, I realized that all of those delusions were about things which had happened in the past, or phantoms and imaginations about the future, along with worries about not wanting to make mistakes in the future. And because I was always trying to find methods for not making mistakes, I created more delusions.

I promised myself that I will not lose myself again in delusions, and that, because today is my entire life, I will live today appreciatively.

Suddenly my body, which before had been very heavy, became light, and to the person whom I first met this morning I could give a true, warm smile.

745. June 6, 1994. Paris

We live in Buddha's (absolute, truth, nothingness) great love and great compassion. But if we do not realize what this great love and great compassion are, our own love becomes dry and we cannot receive love from others. We are then very lonely.

When you want to realize Buddha's great love and great compassion, first you must strive to love others, whether they are good, bad, difficult or ignorant. While striving to do so, your dry love will disappear and you will realize and truly attain what love is.

Remember, the more you do not like others, the more you will not like yourself. But when you love others, you open the space to love yourself.

746. June 7, 1994. Paris

No matter how hard and difficult most people are, when you deal with and treat them warmly and lovingly, they become warm and loving.

Especially people who have suffered a lot, and grown up without much warmth and love, have dry love and are cold. Even if someone deals with them warmly and treats them lovingly, they doubt about such treatment and sneer at it. When people are like that, do not be bothered by their doubting and sneering minds. Instead, continuously give them warmth and love. While you do that, you will learn about the mind of endurance, you will thoroughly attain what love is, and you will also realize what your own mistakes are. Then you will appreciate those doubting and sneering people who gave you this kind of practice.

By continuously dealing with them, those people who were hard before and whose love was dry will learn what love and warmth are. They will come to appreciate you and to know what the true and correct function of human life is.

747. June 8, 1994. Paris

For your work today, make a meticulous schedule for each thing, one by one. And whatever work is unfinished or incorrectly done, finish and/or correct it today.

The reason you could not do your job correctly until now is that you did not have a clear schedule. So take the time to make a thorough schedule for yourself. Once you make the schedule, do not change or doubt it; just proceed. Then without becoming confused you will accomplish what you must.

But do not expect that it will be easy to accomplish what you have to do. When you have difficulty in your work, take that difficulty as your teacher and your practice. Then your accomplishments will benefit others and will make you happy.

748. June 9, 1994. Paris

Dear:

When you need me, it makes me realize my usefulness.

When you do not give me responsibility, I do not know what my duties and functions are.

When you give me responsibility, I know how to appreciate life.

When you give me responsibility, I learn more and have more experience.

When you give me responsibility, you give me the opportunity to make good luck karma.

When you give me responsibility and I accept it and act sincerely, I become successful.

When you give me responsibility and I do my best, you are
>   happy, and then I learn what true happiness is.

Dear:
>   Please give me more responsibility today, and please need
>   me.

P. S. Today is the first of the month (May) by the Chinese calendar. So please be a needed person. Not being a needed person is great sadness and loneliness.

749. June 10, 1994. Paris

When someone asks you for your opinion, do not only answer from what you see through your own eyes and your own opinion. Also, do not sneer at the person if his question is ignorant.

When you think that someone's question is ignorant and you sneer at him, to that degree you are also ignorant and are demeaning yourself. This means that you are indirectly showing off to others that you believe only your own opinions are correct. This kind of action and thought appears because your ego is large and because you think that you are that ego-self.

So when someone asks you for your opinion, whether his question is big, small, ignorant or funny, do not judge it. Always answer others' questions sincerely and with a mind of respect and gratitude towards the person who asks the question.

Remember the theory that when you discard yourself, you earn yourself. This is just like a tree letting go of its fruit which falls onto the ground, germinates there, and eventually grows into a tree that bears fruit. So when someone asks you a question, throw your own opinions away, become one with the person who asked the question, and answer it sincerely. Then you will always be trusted and respected by others. You will be a needed person, and you will always do the correct function in your duties as a human being.

750. June 11, 1994. Paris

Today, be free from doubts.

Having doubts makes you go into a dark cloud. Also, doubting about others wastes a lot of your important energy, causes you to suffer in all kinds of delusions, and makes it easy to lose yourself.

Change that mind of doubting about others into a mind of watching yourself. When you know how to watch yourself and when what you do is clear, then you do not doubt about others. And when you clearly understand cause and effect, then you understand that cheating others is cheating yourself, hurting others is hurting yourself, and trusting others is trusting yourself.

So even if others act in ways that cause you to have doubts about them, practice to trust yourself and to rescue yourself from your doubts.

751. June 12, 1994. Great Britain

When someone who has been given a gift gives it away instead of keeping it, the person who originally gave the gift should not be disappointed. What is important is giving a gift to someone you like; you need not care about where that gift goes afterwards.

When you give everything to those you love and work for them, you need not think that they must receive all of your benefit. What is important is that you work for and give to them.

Caring for a particular person is caring for everyone. When you care for one person, you are caring for ten thousand people; when you give to and care for a particular person 100 percent, you are giving to and caring for everyone.

Saving all sentient beings begins with saving one person.

752. June 13, 1994. Great Britain

When you have a period of separation from those you live with, you discover their importance and value, and you can truly appreciate them.

While you were together, perhaps you often fought one another because of differences of opinion; perhaps you even hated each other at times. But when you have a period of separation, you feel their importance.

So, when you have a problem with your partner, colleague, friend, and so on, leave the place where you are together and have space from one another. Then you will understand each other better.

People live with and associate with others because they are related from their last lives. So when you make that relationship happy and smooth in this life, it will be happy and smooth in your next life, too. Then that happy and smooth relationship will become a non-relationship and you will free one another. When you meet each other again, your relationship will become a correct relationship, and you will truly appreciate and respect one another.

753. June 14, 1994. Great Britain

When you are in a difficult situation and have many problems and worries because you are not clear about what you are doing, you may discover two kinds of friends.

One type of friend always tries to comfort and support you, no matter how much difficulty you are having. Because these friends want to help relieve you from your agonies, they try to find a sincere solution to your problems. They help without saying or boasting that they are helping.

But a second type of friend blames you for being in difficulty and talks about how terrible it is that you have such a situation. They make you feel more fearful and threatened by your difficulty. They do not know how to solve your problems, but they say they are helping and boast about it.

See if you have both of these kinds of people around you. If you do, ignore the people who fit into the second category and do not let them bother you.

There is an old saying, "When wise people want to get rid of a rat, they always show the rat a hole through which to escape." This means that no matter how many mistakes others make, do not demean them or abuse them for their mistakes. Instead, give them space so that they can see themselves and find their way out.

If you want to help people fix their mistakes, first become clear yourself and then comfort them so they do not feel threatened or fearful.

754. June 15, 1994. Paris

Before you could find the correct path out of your suffering, you floundered in your suffering. Because it was so difficult, you fell down, and it felt as though everything was blocked.

But while there, you had hope, and that hope helped you to find the path by which to come out from your suffering. That hope is just like a lamp's light in the darkness.

You took hold of that hope and stood up. Then the suffering disappeared and you could clearly see which path to take — a path much clearer than the one you had been on before. Now you feel very confident and appreciative, and remembering the suffering you had been feeling, you realize that in human life, while in suffering, you must have hope.

Hope shines more and is much stronger for those who practice because practitioners' hope is not for their small I, but is for everyone.

So when you are in difficulty, please have hope. That hope will save you.

755. June 16, 1994. Paris

Even a brilliant diamond easily becomes dusty. So even if you are clear and bright, when you live in the social world, once in a while you become dusty and this makes you confused.

While in confusion, you can make yourself bright and clear only by practicing and by having faith and trust in Buddha (absolute, truth). That mind of faith and trust will release you from confusion.

The dust that makes you confused is never far away; it is always near. So always be careful about what is closest to you.

The Buddha and the devil are also never far away from you; they are both always close by. So when you see Buddha, do not enjoy it too much; and when you see the devil, do not dislike it too much. Whatever you like or dislike too much, that is your dust.

Always remain humble and watch yourself. With humility, make that dust into a lotus flower and wrap yourself with its fragrance.

Then, when you see Buddha what should you do? And when you see the devil, what should you do?

756. June 17, 1994. Frankfurt

Once there were two people who promised to do things in their lives together and who trusted one another. But suddenly one of the two began acting and speaking in ways aimed only at protecting and benefiting himself. Also, he came to worry solely about his own future.

When the other person saw that, she was hugely disappointed and felt so much pity for the other person because he did not understand how lonely he would become and how much failure he would have because of his acting separately. Because he did not even know how ignorant he was being, she felt so sorry for him.

The person who wanted to act separately thought that he was very smart, but he only understood one, not two.

Human beings must live together and for each other. That is the value of human life and is what makes us successful. If we separate ourselves from others and act to protect and benefit only ourselves, this way of thinking and acting make us fail. Those who are successful have become so because they do things for others, and all people who are failures are so because they only think and act for themselves.

It is the same thing in successful relationships: when a husband is devoted to his wife, when a wife is devoted to her husband, when masters are devoted to their students, when students are devoted to their masters, when bosses are devoted to their employees and when employees are devoted to their bosses, these become successful relationships in which everyone benefits.

So if you are wise, do not separate yourself from others in order to benefit yourself. A person who separates from others has a lot of ego and that ego will bring great loneliness.

So let us live for others.

757. June 18, 1994. Frankfurt

When a cow drinks water, the water becomes milk. But when a snake drinks the same water, the water becomes venom.

Even though people receive the same teaching, the more wise people receive teachings, the humbler, softer and better they become. In them you cannot find ego; you can only find the merit they have built up. They make everyone comfortable, and whoever is with them has great joy and happiness.

But the more unwise people receive teachings, the more arrogant they become and their egos shoot up to the sky. In their eyes, there is no one to respect. Even Buddha and the master are seen by them as being just the same as they are or even lower. Because they act and think as though they are the smartest people in the world, they bother others and no one wants to be with them. If others do stay with them, they suffer and want to leave as soon as possible.

My wish is for all practitioners to become wise. I hope that these daily teachings are milk through which you can make yourselves and others healthy.

758. June 19, 1994. Frankfurt

Do not get caught by human beings' forms, speech and actions. See what is beyond their forms, speech and actions. This means seeing the realm of Buddha (nothingness).

When you can see the realm of Buddha, you do not get caught by good or bad; you see good as good and bad as bad. Instead of getting caught by bad, you have the wisdom to fix what is bad. This wisdom eventually eliminates both good and bad, and leads everyone to the realm of Buddha.

Those who cannot see the realm of Buddha always get caught by form, speech and action and so make themselves negative, which then makes others negative as well. Even if they see Buddha, they do not recognize that this is Buddha; they think that what they know — their own negativity — is actually Buddha, and so they can only make everyone suffer.

The eyes of those who truly see Buddha are full of compassion, and their faces shine with love smiles.

759. June 20, 1994. Paris

You who live in Buddha's love:
Why are you so angry and disappointed today and why do
    you frown like that?

Your anger, disappointment and frown are all made by yourself. Do you know that or not?

When you know that, release your anger, forget your disappointment and open your frown.

When we die, our body becomes only a handful of ashes.

You whose ashes will not amount to even one kilo, why do you try to make yourself so high?

Why are you so arrogant?

Why do you show off?

Do not try to make your light-weight self heavy in this life. In truth it is no-self. Do not carry unnecessary burdens with you into your next life.

Give all of yourself to others.

When you can live lightly in this life, everyone will make you happy and everyone will give you presents. Those presents will weigh thousands of kilos, and those thousands of kilos will make you happy and will make you shine, life after life.

P. S. This is a very important teaching.

760. June 21, 1994. Paris

When you see someone who is sick you think to yourself, "I better be careful not to become sick myself." And when you see someone die, you really feel the impermanence of life. But there is one corner of the mind which does not want to admit the possibility of becoming sick and dying; it refuses even to imagine that.

People often think that they will be healthy and will live for a very long time. That ignorant thinking is always present in a corner of their minds, and with that ignorant mind it is difficult for them to get out of the cycle of their egos. Because they do not want to believe the truth, they become negative.

But when you really understand that humans are born, become old, get sick and die, while you are alive you will not make yourself negative. You will enjoy and appreciate your life. You will use this impermanent form to do many good things for others and to make them happy. You will always strive to benefit others.

Then, when you die you will go comfortably, without hindrance. If you can really go comfortably without hindrance and are born in a subsequent life, you return with lots of luck on your shoulders and with happiness always close by.

Today, let us not make others angry.

Today, let us not become jealous if someone else is doing better than we are.

Today, let us not poke or blame others for their mistakes.

Today, as much as possible, let us make others comfortable.

Today, let us do our duties one hundred percent.

761. June 22, 1994. Paris

Today, check your personality and try to improve it. When you check your personality, sort out the good and bad points. Keep the good points and strive to eliminate the bad points.

For example:
1) If it is in your personality to be too impatient and rushed, go in the direction of becoming more patient and slower.

2) If it is in your personality to complain about others, go in the direction of complimenting others.
3) If it is in your personality to doubt about others, go in the direction of understanding others.
4) If it is in your personality not to trust others, go in the direction of trusting others.
5) Whatever bad you see, go in the direction of changing it into being good.
6) If it is in your personality to see things as being ugly, go in the direction of thinking that things are okay.
7) If you think that someone else is not suitable for you, go in the direction of thinking that you have a strong connection with that person.
8) If you have a frowning face, go in the direction of changing it into a smiling face.

Today, strongly strive to better your personality. The mind and action of striving will make you change, and while changing you will see yourself more clearly.

Human beings make their own karma and destiny. So when they better their personalities they become successful and happy, and furthermore make themselves into Buddhas.

Remember, Shakyamuni Buddha did not become a Buddha for free. Through strongly striving and practicing, he bettered himself and that is why he attained Buddhahood and became a Buddha himself.

Today, let us not make others angry.

Today, let us not become jealous if someone else is doing better than we are.

Today, let us not poke or blame others for their mistakes.

Today, as much as possible let us make others comfortable.

Today, let us do our duties 100 percent.

762. June 23, 1994. Paris

The mind which expects others' help;

The mind which would like to have others' things;

The mind which would like to be respected by others;

These minds make you negative.

When you do not get these things from others:

That is the seed of becoming disappointed in others;

That is the seed of becoming jealous of others;

That is the seed of becoming angry at others.

So:

Change the mind which expects others' help into the mind which first helps others;

Change the mind which wants others' things into the mind of first offering to others;

Change the mind which would like to be respected by others into the mind which first respects others.

When you do these things, your mind becomes positive and that positive mind makes no-mind and that no-mind emancipates you.

Today, let us not make others angry.

Today, let us not become jealous if someone else is doing better than we are.

Today, let us not poke or blame others for their mistakes.

Today, as much as possible let us make others comfortable.

Today, let us do our duties 100 percent.

763. June 24, 1994. Paris

Whatever difficulty comes your way, do not be afraid of it, do not get disappointed by it, do not become angry because of it, and do not rush into trying to solve it. When difficulties arise, breathe deeply, repeat the mantra, and say to yourself:

1) I will take care of this difficulty in a beautiful way.
2) I will take care of this difficulty with love and compassion.
3) No matter how big a difficulty it is, I will make it small and overcome it.

Then, wisdom of a depth you never even imagined will appear and your difficulty will lead you to a realization. You will learn many things, and you will attain the power of trusting yourself.

A difficult situation can be an easy situation, and an easy situation can be a difficult situation. But do not think of a particular situation as being either difficult or easy. When you do your duties 100 percent, there are no difficult or easy situations. Then whatever you do is solid and clear and no one can hinder or bother you.

Today, let us not make others angry.

Today, let us not become jealous if someone else is doing better than we are.

Today, let us not poke or blame others for their mistakes.

Today, as much as possible let us make others comfortable.
Today, let us do our duties 100 percent.

764. June 25, 1994. Paris

The mind which trusts others is a happy mind. When you have a person whom you trust, that person is the happiest person. The mind which trusts others does not have ego and is a humble mind.

Having someone whom you trust happens because you did a lot of bodhisattva actions in your previous life. In the mind that trusts others, there is beauty, love and compassion. When you have someone whom you trust, you will never be poor; you will always live in prosperity.

If you want to have a mind which trusts others, and a person whom you can trust, first practice to trust others. And while practicing, find yourself. When you find yourself, that self can trust the non-self and then you can trust many other people.

765. June 26, 1994. Paris

Just as one finds medicines in pain, one finds true happiness in suffering.

If you are not afraid of pain and suffering and do not lose yourself in health and happiness, no one can make you suffer and wherever you go you will always make others happy and benefit them. You will then protect yourself, but not burden others. And if you can give others the one square meter of space you occupy, then you are a Buddha and a bodhisattva.

If you should see such a person, you must give him a sincere *hapchang*.

766. June 27, 1994. Paris

For such a long time, living in fear and worry,
Wanting to have such a good life,
Never resting for even a single day,
Always running, running,
And then coming here today.
The body is already worn out,
The mind is not comfortable,
There are so many things to take care of.

This is life for most human beings. But why do we have to live in fears and worries, and why do we have to chase after a good life?

It is so that in human life, suffering always comes before we can begin living an appreciative and successful life. That is pitiful and makes people anxious.

But when we believe in Buddha (absolute, truth) and in practicing, our fears and worries change into peacefulness, comfort and relaxation. New energy flows into our worn out bodies, and we appreciate our existence today. Then we do not doubt about our jobs and we act out of gratitude.

767. June 28, 1994. Paris

We come from the place of nothingness, but we have a form of something; and this form of something is always looking for something. For this reason, we can even come close to losing our form of something. But one morning, all of a sudden we wake up and say, "This is not the correct path."

The correct path is to look for nothingness with our form of something. When we realize this, we change our direction and go into nothingness. Then,

> We do not become complicated or difficult;
> We do not have anything to cover up;
> We do not have to lie;
> We do not have to show off;
> We do not have to become angry;
> We do not have to be jealous; and,
> We do not have to expect anything from others.
> It is so comfortable. Why did we not realize this earlier?
> True thanks to the Buddha, thanks to the Dharma, and thanks to the master.
> Thank you, thank you, thank you.

768. June 29, 1994. Honolulu

When you tell a not-so-good person that he is not so good, he becomes worse. When you tell a good person that he is good, he becomes better.

Let us not discriminate about people and judge what they do. Whether they are good or not-so- good, try to deal with everyone equally but give more attention to those who are not so good.

The reason people are not so good is that, due to their karma, they did not meet the right person who could give them great love and compassion. They only met people who are conditional, and so they became not-so-good through associating with them.

No matter how not-so-good people are, when you treat them truly, and you sincerely give them great love, great compassion, space, and a chance, then they will change and they can even become much better than those who were good from the beginning.

Let us not be picky about good or not-so-good, and instead try to offer ourselves more to others.

769. June 30, 1994. Honolulu

The mind which wants to compete with others and live better than them has many good points which can build you up. But if you live with that kind of mind, even if you become successful in the future, that success will become empty. At the same time, all of your mistakes will appear and you will dirty yourself. After succeeding, suffering will follow.

But if you can change the mind which wants to compete with and live better than others into the mind which wants to help and serve others, even though it may take a little longer, you will succeed. And after succeeding, unexpected satisfaction and true happiness will follow.

The mind which wants to help and serve others comes from the realm of Buddha (absolute, truth, nothingness). Do not forget that in that mind, there is unlimited supernatural penetration power.

770. July 1, 1994. Honolulu

Try to plan what kind of life you want to live from today on. Write down your plans, wishes and how long you would like to live in this world.

For those of you who would like to show me your plans and wishes, please write or fax a letter to Hawaii. I hope you all make great plans and wishes; I will put a lot of effort and energy into them.

771. July 2, 1994. Honolulu

I hope all of you can appreciate the remainder of this year. I also hope that during this coming half-year you accomplish whatever things you began, planned and practiced for in the past six months, and that you realize many things.

According to my perception, the energy for the second half of this year will most likely be settled. Whatever the reasons you could not find happiness in the first six months, I hope you can find happiness from now on.

Remember that after a hurricane there is always a beautiful, calm ocean, and that after the storm there is always a beautiful, clear sky. Find hope in difficulty and do not to lose yourself in happiness. Then you can have a good day, every day.

772. July 3, 1994. Honolulu

Depending upon what kind of method we use, we are able to accomplish things or we fail. Because we do not want to fail, we worry and agonize about finding the correct method.

We try to find the correct method through knowledge and through our experience. But if we find the correct method through them, it is still hard to escape the world of opposites; and even if we do escape the world of opposites, the method discovered through knowledge and experience is not clear afterwards.

When we find the right method through wisdom, it may not seem to be correct at the beginning, but as time goes by this method shines, becomes successful and benefits everybody. Correct wisdom comes from the place of nothingness.

When you want to find the correct method:
1) Forget about the subject,
2) Relax,
3) Be tranquil,
4) Depend on the Dharma,
5) Depend upon the teachings, and
6) Depend upon the practice.

Then, wisdom will appear from the place of nothingness, this wisdom will lead you to the correct path, and this path will make you appreciate yourself and others.

773. July 4, 1994. Honolulu

Each human being's body and mind has its individual karma, according to which each person acts, thinks and speaks. When one's body and mind disappear, one's action and speech remain, but as time goes by they also disappear. However, if one's speech and action aimed for the benefit of everyone, they exist eternally.

Appearing, disappearing, reappearing and disappearing again — this is the way of human beings' bodies and minds. They are impermanent. So according to how you use your impermanent body and mind, life changes. When you use them in a good way, you have a good life; and when you use them in a bad way, you have a bad life.

But when you use your body and mind for others, unhindered by either appearing or disappearing, you will have an eternally shining life and you will be able to shape your karma as you wish. Then, if you want to return to this world, you will return; and if you want to disappear, you will disappear. It is just like always having a seat on the airplane without having to make a ticket reservation. You are an eternal traveler, and wherever you go you always enjoy life and live an infinite, permanent life.

774. July 5, 1994. Honolulu

In every human being's mind there is beauty. But according to whether one's karma is light or heavy, that beauty either appears or does not appear.

People who have a lot of karma do not even know what beauty is, and so they live life without it. And because they do not know what beauty is, they make themselves and others suffer.

Only those who know what beauty is can exemplify beauty. Many people automatically follow, believe and have faith in those who know what beauty is and who exemplify it.

No matter how strong the desire for respect and an elevated position in life is, those who do not know what beauty is will not receive respect and a high position.

Beauty comes from before knowledge and before thinking. It is difficult to explain beauty through speech and words, but when you can throw your small self away and lower yourself, beauty appears; and when you think about others and act for others, beauty appears through you.

775. July 6, 1994. Honolulu

While living in this world, if there is nothing to take revenge upon, no complaints to be heard from others, and no enemies to make, you can live quietly. This is a very comfortable life. But even if revenge is taken, complaints are heard from others, and enemies are made, if we go onto the correct path, whatever revenge, complaints and enemies there were can be changed into harmonizing with others, complimenting others, and forming friendships.

The correct path is to benefit everyone. Being on the path of benefiting everyone is difficult at first, but with time you become very appreciative of it. Having appreciation means that wherever you go and whatever you do, your action disappears and leaves no trace behind with anyone.

If you truly do things for others without showing it and just help them, that action shines forever. But if in your action something shows, even if you acted to help and benefit others, others may come to complain about it.

776. July 7, 1994. Honolulu

When one's mind is very tightly locked, one suffers in loneliness, cannot open up, and only waits for someone to come. But if someone does not come, one blames others and easily wastes the day in unnecessary depression.

From now on we must use our minds and energy to open up. Widely open up that mind which was tightly closed and show yourself to others; do not be ashamed of yourself and do not worry about whether you are good or bad. By showing yourself to others, you will come to understand thoroughly what is good and what is bad.

When you show yourself to others, they will also open their doors and will show themselves to you. When you show yourselves to each other, there is nothing left and then those nothings become friends with one another. In this pace of joined nothings, true love flows, and with that true love, you protect and truly understand each other.

777. July 8, 1994. Honolulu

A guitar has many strings, each of which makes a different sound.

Each problem that we have in our lives seems to be similar, but they are all different. Also, when we finish one problem, another one is always waiting for us. So we always have many things to do and we cannot rest.

When you feel that you have so many things to do and cannot rest, stress is always the first thing to come. At that time, do not allow yourself to become stressed by all the things you have to do, do not feel that they are difficult, and do not try to escape from what you must do. Instead, think of all that you have to do as being interesting, and appreciate having the duties that have been given to you.

Have endurance and patience, just like when you steadily untangle a knot, one move at a time. Then, while untangling your difficulties and carrying out your duties, you will be filled with happiness; and no matter how many things you have to do, you can always relax.

When you can work in a relaxed way, the feeling that you have too many things to do disappears. And when you can work without the feeling that there are too many things to do, even though you end up erecting a Mount Sumeru it does not seem as though you did so. And even if you climb up and down the mountain many times a day with bare feet, you do not feel as though it was difficult, and all that remains from going up and down many times are your drops of sweat.

778. July 9, 1994. Honolulu

When parents raise their children, they should not expect their children to be like themselves, to be better than they are, or to accomplish whatever they did not accomplish in their own lives. When parents raise their children with many wishes and expectations and their children do not fulfill those wishes and expectations, the parents blame their children. Then they do not have a good relationship with each other, and a lot of sadness and suffering is created.

When parents raise their children, they must eliminate their mind of expectations and worry and just appreciate that they have children to raise. They should become best friends with their children and truly help them as truthful friends.

When children think of their parents as their true friends, everything becomes fantastic.

779. July 10, 1994. Honolulu

In order to accomplish their goals, some people strive a lot and sometimes even put their whole life into their striving. Ordinary people cannot comprehend the concentration of those who really want to accomplish a goal. But with that concentration, people can often accomplish remarkable things.

You must think very seriously about your goal before setting out to accomplish it. Does your goal come from your emotions and feelings? Is it to be victorious over, rule or take revenge upon others? That kind of goal always hurts oneself and others.

A true goal has a mind of sacrifice in it, is more for others than for oneself, and is ultimately for all sentient beings. That kind of goal frees the person who has it and also frees others.

780. July 11, 1994. Honolulu

People who think that they are always right lose many things and always live in their own world of attachment. They cannot see or understand others, and when things do not go well they blame others and the way the whole world is, trapping themselves in suffering.

People who are truly right find their correctness through others and discover happiness through others' comfortable minds. They enjoy true happiness with others.

781. July 12, 1994. Honolulu

When someone needs you, help that person sincerely and appreciate that another person needs you. The fact that someone needs you means that you have value.

So when someone needs you, do not think that they are trying to use you. If you avoid the opportunity presented by someone needing you, then in the future nobody will need you anymore. A person who is not needed by others always becomes lonely and loses his value as a human being.

All opportunities to do things for others and jobs which are given to you are situations in which you are needed by others. So work sincerely and with vigor, and do not complain when you have many things to do. The more things you have to do, the more diligently you must work. When you do your work diligently, thinking that you have too much to do will disappear and you will become a person who is truly needed by others. In this way, you find true appreciation for being a human being.

782. July 13, 1994. Honolulu

We can say that human life is interesting. But on the other hand, we cannot really say that it is interesting.

Most human beings appear in this world and while living they burden others, make difficulties for others, and become greatly indebted to others. Then they again leave their bodies to nature and disappear, leaving this world.

Whether appearing and disappearing, coming and going, and the endlessly far journey of human life are interesting or not, when one comes to this world one must live; and when one must go from this world, one must go. Given this, you can think that coming and going and living are interesting, but the suffering that appears with them is not interesting.

So we may say that the long journey itself is interesting. But it is that very interest itself which is actually most interesting.

Then, where does suffering exist?

P. S. *This is a puzzle teaching.*

783. July 14, 1994. Honolulu

When those who are unwise receive credit from and are trusted by others, they easily neglect their responsibilities and think that they have already accomplished what they had to accomplish.

When wise persons receive credit from and are trusted by others, they understand the important and heavy responsibility they have and work much more vigorously than before.

When unwise people receive credit from and are trusted by others, their egos become bigger and because of this they lose the credit and trust they had received from others.

The more wise people receive credit from and are trusted by others, the humbler they become, and with that humility they find their original place. In this original place, they make themselves shine, and whoever sees them becomes happy.

784. July 15, 1994. Honolulu

If you want to help someone today, do not help whoever is in front of them. Rather, help whoever is behind them. This means that when you help others, do not show that you are helping. This is how to find correct ways of helping others and finding true wisdom.

When you help others in a showy way, your ego grows larger. But when you help others in ways that are not showy, your humility grows larger. When your humility grows, you are eliminating your karma.

So if there is someone you want to help, seriously think about how you can help them. In that moment, while thinking about how to help others, your delusion changes into wisdom, and this wisdom brings power which you did not even know of before. In that power you find your true I and your true I makes you understand why you have to help first those who are not in front of someone, but behind them.

785. July 16, 1994. Honolulu

You keep the mind wide and comfortable, but then you get caught by a small and unimportant matter and the wide and comfortable mind disappears. Because you know that it was a small and unimportant matter and you see that you got caught by it, your mind becomes even more uncomfortable and you realize that your mind is still narrow. It makes you feel shameful and causes you to have a headache.

At this kind of time, put your mind into the direction of forgetting the whole thing and remember: we are living in the nothingness.

Getting caught by small, little things happens because things do not go exactly how you want. But remember: since you do not know your own mind, how can you expect things to always go how you want? That expectation is ignorant and causes us to get caught by even small, little things. So put everything into nothingness and go into nothingness. Then there are no small or large matters to get caught by, there is nothing to be ashamed of, and your coursing along the path of your life is comfortable.

786. July 17, 1994. Honolulu

When there is strong wind and rain, flowers that were raised in a greenhouse and then put outside easily shrivel and may even die. But for flowers that have grown in open fields, the more wind and rain there are, the healthier and more beautiful they become.

Human beings are similar to this. When those who have grown up in very good, protected and comfortable environments come into difficulty, they fall down and really suffer because of it. But those who grew up in difficult situations are not afraid of difficulty and are readily able to overcome adversity.

But whether practice people grew up in good or difficult situations, with the power of practice they overcome all difficulties and engage them as teachings. They appreciate whatever situations come their way and, without fear or difficulty, welcome each day with happiness.

787. July 18, 1994. Honolulu

When you accomplish what you really want, it is easy to become attached to your accomplishment, and because of this greed appears. With greed, jealousy easily appears and that jealousy creates many fantasies and delusions. It is then difficult to judge the situation you are in clearly, and your senses turn ignorant. Those ignorant senses lead you into making many mistakes that hurt you as well as others.

Your accomplishment is the result of your striving and effort, and that is why accomplishing what you want feels so important and precious. It is due to this feeling of importance and preciousness that you so deeply attach to your accomplishment.

But practice people: even if you accomplish what you really want and this feels important and precious to you, do not attach to your accomplishment. Simply appreciate your accomplishment. Use it as a foundation and set your sights on something higher than what you have just achieved. Then strive to reach that goal and forget about your previous accomplishments.

788. July 19, 1994. Honolulu

In the mountains, flowers are blooming; in the oceans, fish are swimming; in the sky, cloud-flowers are floating; and across the land, many fruits and vegetables are ripening.

This world is a beautiful place. Since we are living in this beautiful world, why do we have difficulties and why do we suffer? The reason is that we do not see the world clearly. That is why.

If you want to see the world clearly, do not attach to the color and shape of the flower that is blooming in the mountains; do not discriminate between the high and low waves the fish make when swimming in the ocean; do not blame the cloud-flower in the sky for floating high or low or separately from others; and do not complain that the fruits and vegetables growing in the land are yellow or green or too many or too few.

Then you can see the world clearly, and even if a difficult situation appears, you can deal with it comfortably. Suffering then changes into happiness.

789. July 20, 1994. Honolulu

Nirvana and the present life seem to be far apart from each other, but they are not; they are very close together. But when you have a lot of karma in this life, even though nirvana and the present life are very close together, they seem to be very distant from one another.

Also, when you have a lot of heavy karma, even though you are in nirvana, you do not know how to enjoy it. That is because you did not accomplish the job you were supposed to accomplish.

In the world of karma, bad karma is afraid of nirvana. But good karma thinks of nirvana as a resort and enjoys it.

When you have a lot of good karma, wherever you go, whether to nirvana or to this present life, you are happy. And wherever you go, others greet you with love and as someone who is needed.

790. July 21, 1994. Honolulu

Today, move your body and keep busy. Try to complete whatever unfinished work you have from before. But if you do not have anything you must do, then clean and arrange your personal space. Wash whatever is dirty, give away those things that you no longer need but someone else can use, and organize and wash your clothes. Make the space all around you very clean.

Then at night, completely rest, and tomorrow morning begin the next day.

791. July 22, 1994. Honolulu

When feelings inside the body and feelings outside of the body separate, it is as though one is floating in the air; one does not know which feelings to choose and one suffers for a while.

When feelings inside of the body are stronger than those outside of the body, one comes back and settles into one's body. But when feelings outside of the body are stronger than those inside of the body, one forgets one's body and floats around homelessly. Then one must find one's own karma. When one finds one's own karma, one then reappears in a new form.

Being born, getting old, falling sick and dying is a law from which nobody can escape. If you try to escape from it, then instead of helping sentient beings you ruin them.

When you know the law of being born, getting old, falling sick and dying, you can respect the exquisiteness of that process without having any suffering, and while immersed in that process, you can find the real truth without having any difficulty.

792. July 23, 1994. Honolulu

Although you are falling ill, do not feel sick and do not think of being sick as suffering. Rather, think that you are getting sick because you are alive. When you think that way, your becoming ill functions as correct medicine, and that correct medicine eliminates sickness and suffering.

Through your sickness, it is possible to know how to take care of and keep your body correctly. That wisdom turns into medicine that can be used to help other people who are ill. You can even become a living medicine for people who are not well, truly and sincerely helping many others through your experience.

793. July 24, 1994. Honolulu

Human beings use whatever amount of energy they have. But sometimes, in certain situations, they surprise themselves by how much energy they have. The reason for their surprise is that they only know what they can do, and they do not expect to be able to do more than that. In fact, they do not even want to know that they can do much more.

But people who realize nothingness (Buddha, absolute, truth) and who know its power do not think of their own energy as being powerful. They see that their energy is just to keep their bodily "motor" running and realize that all of their power is not coming from their body but rather from nothingness.

If people like this have a difficult situation and overcome it, they do not say that it was them who did so; they just appreciate and depend upon the power of nothingness and do their duties. Whether there is a lot or a little bit of work to be done, they just do it; and whatever duties are given to them, they handle them sincerely and with vigor.

794. July 25, 1994. Honolulu

When you are comfortable and bright, it seems that everything is comfortable and bright.

When you are not comfortable or bright, it seems that everything is not comfortable or bright, and you see everything as being dark.

When you do things in darkness, you cannot do them correctly; you make many mistakes, thus making yourself and others suffer.

So first make yourself comfortable. Even if you are not in a comfortable situation, strive to become comfortable. Your striving will bring you comfort and will give birth to wisdom.

But remember, the most comfortable place is not in the comfortable place. It is beyond comfort and discomfort.

795. July 26, 1994. Honolulu

The foundation of happiness must come from the place of no-place. But to find the place of no-place, you must go through much suffering because eliminating what you have (karma, sensations, feelings, greed, desire, jealousy, anger, ego) is very difficult. When those things are eliminated, then you will know the place of no-place.

When you begin to eliminate what you have, it seems as though you are losing yourself, and so it is difficult to imagine that you will eliminate all those things. But as they diminish, one by one, you will discover something about karma, sensations, feelings, greed, desire, jealousy, anger and ego which you never knew before, and they will no longer block you.

When you accomplish this, you will have eternal happiness within the place of no-place.

796. July 27, 1994. Honolulu

When a beautiful hand writes beautiful words on white paper, those words become beautiful, the meaning of what is written becomes beautiful, and the mind of the person who reads them becomes beautiful. That beautiful mind makes beautiful speech; that beautiful speech makes beautiful thinking; that beautiful thinking makes beautiful action; and that beautiful action makes a beautiful hand.

That beautiful hand is not only writing the words, but is also touching sentient beings' minds and bodies and eliminating their suffering. Whenever that hand touches them, it makes happiness and comfort. That hand is the hand of all Buddhas and bodhisattvas.

This Buddha- and bodhisattva-hand and your hand, are they the same or are they different?

How are you? Please be happy today.

797. July 28, 1994. Honolulu

Everything is created by the mind alone. So when we do not think, there is no thinking, and when we want to forget something, we can forget it. But when there is something in front of us, even if we want to forget it, it is difficult to do so.

When you try to like a person whom you do not like, but he or she continues to do things that you dislike, it is difficult to like this person. Also, even if this person does good actions which you like, it is difficult to see them as likable actions.

At that kind of time, do not try to like the person whom you do not like, and also do not think that it is difficult to like that person. Just realize that all of the sentient beings who are covered by ignorance are pitiable and that it is because they are covered by ignorance that they make each other suffer.

Also realize that in clarity there are neither good nor bad, like nor dislike. Simply strive to make yourself bright and clear.

798. July 29, 1994. Honolulu

When you are in an urgent and important situation, do not get caught and hung up by it, and do not lose your time and space. When you get caught by it and lose yourself, you regret it afterwards.

The more urgent and important the situation you are in, the more you must have a mind which has time and space. That way you can take care of your things very well, and after accomplishing them you will not receive any negative side effects.

Everything exists and is accomplished within time and space. When you can freely use time and space, true I exists and that true I shines and is bright when time and space are transcended.

799. July 30, 1994. Honolulu

If you see bad things, do not look at them in a bad way.

If you see ugly things, do not look at them in an ugly way.

If you hear a bad story, do not hear it in a bad way.

Rather than seeing bad things in a bad way, strive to see them in a good way.

Rather than looking at ugly things in an ugly way, strive to see them in a beautiful way.

Rather than hearing a bad story in a bad way, strive to understand and hear it in a good way.

Then the bad and ugly things and the bad stories will be transformed and they will help you, will aim you toward realization, and you will become true friends with the true I which does not have good or bad.

Then you can follow as the wind blows and as the waves undulate, and you will have a boredom-free, interesting journey, life after life.

800. July 31, 1994. Honolulu

Negative people's and positive people's original place and substance are the same. That original place and substance is a true, bright, really clear, clear place which does not get tainted. It is difficult to express it through language; it is such a clean, pure and beautiful place.

Because positive people know a little bit about their original place and substance, they make positive actions and positive karma, and thus become positive people.

Because negative people do not yet know their original place and substance, they do not know how to act correctly or how to make correct karma, and that is why they become negative people.

If you have a little patience and endurance in dealing with those people who are negative, treating them as though they were positive people, you will at first find it difficult to penetrate them and you may even get a problem, but as time passes they will change into positive people who can even be much better and more trustworthy than people who were positive to begin with.

801. August 1, 1994. Honolulu

Life is just like a long journey during which one makes a short, relaxed stopover here, and then continues on again.

But if the path of one's journey is not clear, even though you are supposed to relax here before going on, you cannot; and even though you are on the move to somewhere else, you do not know where.

Because you are not clear about that, even though you come back to the same path many times, you cannot distinguish one time from the next, and you make the same mistakes over and over again. Because of that, you suffer, spinning around as if in a whirlpool, unable to relax at all, and then go again.

This life is a stopover during which to relax. But the question is how to spend your time here appreciatively. The ways to spend time appreciatively are:

1) Not to make others suffer because of yourself.
2) Not to bother others because of yourself.
3) To be a needed person for others.

If you act in these ways, you can spend this life appreciatively, you can relax, and at the same time the path of the journey will become clear. Then you will discover where to go to, and whenever you return again you will have an appreciative, new life each time. At the same time, you will come and go without attachments and will enjoy each life, life after life.

802. August 2, 1994. Honolulu

Today, see that self which is meditating; see that self which is doing prostrations; see where that self comes from; and see where that self is going.

When you can see that self which is meditating, at that moment, 84,000 delusions disappear. When you can see that self which is doing prostrations, at that moment, ego disappears. When you realize where that self comes from, at that moment, you can wake-up from ignorance and stop making the same mistakes. When you know where that self is going, at that moment, greed, jealousies and anger disappear.

When you realize these things and do not make anything at all, then you can see me even though my form is not visible to you, and you can have a true conversation with me.

In true conversation, we are protecting each other. My teaching comes through your speech, your speech expresses my teaching, and even though you do not see my form we are never separate.

Na Mu Kwan Se Um Bo Sal,
Na Mu So Ga Mo Ni Bul,
Chong Gak Mio Poep Yon Hwa Kyong.

803. August 3, 1994. Honolulu

Perfectionists have gaps, and it is in order to cover these gaps that they want to be ever more of a perfectionist and impress others with their perfectionism.

People who do not have gaps have a lot of sympathy and compassion, and instead of being perfectionists, they make mistakes once in a while. But those mistakes are erased by the love they receive from others.

But if perfectionists can fill their gaps with true love, they can become Buddhas who realize that their perfectionism must come from others. Then, continuously doing bodhisattva actions, unhindered by others' good, bad, mistakes or correctness, they will do whatever jobs are given to them vigorously and diligently. Without realizing it, they will automatically become perfect people.

804. August 4, 1994. Honolulu

A long time ago, there was a young man who heard about a famous master and went on a long journey to meet him. Finally, he found the temple where the master was staying.

At that time, the master was working in the fields with his students and so the young man thought that the master was just one of the workers. He approached the master and asked, "I am looking for the famous master. Do you know where he is?"

In answer, the master said, "In this plot, potatoes are growing, and in that plot, carrots."

Hearing this, the young man felt ridiculous. He became angry and responded brusquely. "Why do you give me such a ridiculous answer? I asked you where the master is."

The master started laughing, "Ha, ha, ha, ha," and said, "I am sorry that I gave you such a ridiculous answer. Among those people over there is someone who can help you. Go find the master there."

Then, even though he felt ridiculous, the young man went to talk to the group of people the master had pointed out. He approached one person there and said, "Where is the master? I asked that old man over there and he only said, 'In this plot, potatoes are growing, and in that plot, carrots.' After that, he told me to ask you all. So please answer me, where is the master?"

The person he asked smiled and said, "You already had a great teaching from the master, but you have failed to penetrate his meaning, so how can I help you?"

The young man felt ashamed that he had not recognized the master and his great teaching, and that he had become angry at him.

But he had a great question: "Why did the master say, 'In this plot potatoes are growing, and in that plot, carrots,' when I asked where the master is? And why, afterwards, did he say to find the master in the group of people?" He was completely stuck.

So my question today is: if you were the young man, what would you say is the meaning of "in this plot potatoes are growing, and in that plot, carrots"? And what would you say is the meaning of "find the master in the group of people"?

805. August 5, 1994. Honolulu

Good and smart people who are around an ignorant person can become bad people and can lose their good reputations and credit with others. Also, because good and smart people do not want to deal with an ignorant person, they go away from him. But because that ignorant person speaks so badly about the people who left, others believe that the good and smart people are the ones who are bad.

Never only believe your ears and do not doubt your eyes. Be clear yourself so that you can see and hear clearly. Then you can judge others.

A clear person hears with his eyes and sees with his ears, and doing so does not become attached to or caught by any ignorant person's speech or actions.

The deeper your path of practice becomes, the more clearly you can see right and wrong. But even if you see clearly, do not get caught or bothered by what you see and hear. Just go straight.

806. August 6, 1994. Yun Hwa Dharma Sah

When you cannot deal in a soft way with someone you do not like, more situations will appear that are disagreeable to you. Also, sometimes when there is someone you dislike and you nevertheless try to be nice, their speech and actions are so ignorant that your mind of trying to be nice disappears. You end up disliking them more, and this disliking mind may turn into hating mind.

But remember, people whom you dislike are always connected with your own karma, and the reason you dislike them is that you have gotten caught by your own karma. In order to eliminate that karma, practice to eliminate your disliking mind, raise the mind of compassion as high as you can, and have pity for both yourself and those you dislike. Then that disliking mind will disappear and you will no longer get caught by people you did not like. At the same time, you will be able to deal with them comfortably, and in that comfortable mind you will find clarity. With that clarity you will make a better relationship with those you have disliked, each of those relationships will become a no-relationship, and you will be free from both yourself and others.

807. August 7, 1994. Yun Hwa Dharma Sah

Today is the first day of the second half of the year by the Chinese calendar. Whatever you did not accomplish during the first half of the year, this is the month during which you can accomplish those things.

This month has many special events. Especially important are the ceremonies for the Ancestors and for Seven Stars Day, which is the day commemorating the meeting of true lovers. Because we want our wishes to come true, we make ceremonies for our ancestors and for others.

Do not think about yourself; this is the month during which, if you vigorously do good things for others, your own wishes will automatically come true and you will surprise yourself.

This month, show deep appreciation for your ancestors, your parents, and whoever is related and connected with you; work hard for and help all the people you know.

808. August 8, 1994. Yun Hwa Dharma Sah

Even if you know and realize the place of Buddha, it is difficult to get out from whatever karma you made before; it takes time to dissolve our karma.

Each time you get out from your own karma, you see what kind of karma you had and how ignorant you were. Because of that, you feel ashamed. But when you know how ignorant you were and you feel ashamed because of it, then that ignorant karma disappears. And when you see the ignorance of the people you are connected with karmically and how they act, you see how valuable your realization is.

After this realization, your job is to help and save the people you know who are still in ignorance; you will thoroughly understand that that is your true job. But while you help and save the people who are in ignorance, because it is easy for your old habits and karma to reappear, you must be careful not to again fall into ignorance yourself.

809. August 9, 1994. Yun Hwa Dharma Sah

While in the karma world, trying to know the non-self world and the place of Buddha is a great honor and is very special.

Karma I only sees with the eyes, hears with the ears, touches with the hands, and thinks that this is the true world. The eyes, ears and hands of karma I are not the truth, but karma I does not believe this. That is why karma I gets caught by what it sees, hears and touches. Also, when in the karma I, you are always running around, and for this reason it is difficult to imagine that there is a non-self world.

When this ignorant kind of karma I tries to know the non-self world, it has a lot of difficulty at the beginning. It is just like a tiger used to eating meat that eats grass, or a cow used to eating grass that eats meat; it is difficult for the tiger to digest the grass and for the cow to digest meat. But if human beings who are used to eating vegetables eat meat, they can digest it; and if human beings who are used to eating meat eat vegetables, they can digest that. Human beings have this kind of flexible body.

When human beings make up their minds to do something, they can conquer any difficulties or obstacles which appear along the way, and they can attain the non-self world and become a Buddha.

Trying to know the non-self world is already going into the non-self world and becoming a Buddha oneself. That is why it is a great honor and a very special thing to try to know the non-self world and the place of Buddha.

810. August 10, 1994. Yun Hwa Dharma Sah

When you can see yourself, you can see true I. But when you cannot see yourself, and you try to see true I, what you see is nothing but an imagination.

The face you see reflected in a mirror is made from the four elements and karma. When you look at that face and it is in shadow and is not bright, it is that much harder for you to see or even imagine true I. But when the face reflected in the mirror is bright, and both ugliness and beauty disappear, you can see true I. That true I always sees your face, that true I makes that face either beautiful or ugly, and that face makes others happy, gives them peace, and makes their minds beautiful.

True I always watches you so you do not get caught by either negativity or positivity; it shows you the correct function of your face. When you know the correct function of your face, you will more greatly appreciate having this present form and you will know how to eternally keep form's true beauty.

811. August 11, 1994. Yun Hwa Dharma Sah

Buddha (true I) always sees us, but because we are stuck in the form world it is difficult for us to see Buddha.

In order to see Buddha, it is as though we have to climb many mountains, cross many rivers and search in all directions. But still we cannot see Buddha, and we become disappointed and give up searching.

But one morning I am awakened by the sound of the rooster crowing: in the east where the sun is rising, Buddha sees me and smiles at me; in the wind from the west, Buddha tells me that he loves me; in the sound of the birds in the north, Buddha tells me that this is true; and in the ocean in the south, Buddha tells me to do many bodhisattva actions and to make everyone happy.

Na Mu Kwan Se Um Bo Sal,
Na Mu So Ga Mo Ni Bul,
Chong Gak Mio Poep Yon Hwa Kyong.

812. August 12, 1994. Yun Hwa Dharma Sah

From outside, someone called, "(name)". At that moment, the six gates simultaneously responded, "Yes," and an innocent baby bodhisattva was just about to come out. But the ugly gate guard of the six gates said, "No! You are not ready to exit from these gates yet. I will go out instead." So the ugly gate guard said, "Yes" and went out.

The innocent baby bodhisattva felt hurt, but she endured her pain and said to herself, "When I become bigger that ugly looking gate guard will not be able to block me."

As time went by the innocent baby bodhisattva grew up, and one morning someone called, "(name)". The innocent bodhisattva strongly answered, "Yes!" and immediately ran out. The ugly gate guard tried to stop her but he could not and fell down.

After exiting the six gates, the innocent bodhisattva felt so good and overjoyed, and yelled, "The sky is blue, the tree is green, the flower is red! I love you truly. Oh you who call me, you are so beautiful. I am yours. How may I help you?"

813. August 13, 1994. Yun Hwa Dharma Sah

Today is Seven Stars Day, which is the day when lovers meet one another and also wishes-come- true day.

Today is the day to make others happy and benefit them. The reason is that in happy mind is bodhisattva mind; and bodhisattva mind is for others, to benefit them and make them happy. So with that mind, do many bodhisattva-actions for others.

To do bodhisattva-actions is to find true I. To be in true I is to live a free, unhindered life.

Everybody, I hope that all your wishes come true!

814. August 14, 1994. Yun Hwa Dharma Sah

Being overly kind to people makes them feel burdened and also causes them to have doubts about the person who is acting in an overly kind manner. But when kindness comes from the truth, whether it seems to have been too much or too little, it always makes others comfortable and happy.

Being overly kind comes from having conditions, and not being kind comes from getting caught by one's own conditions.

Even if it sometimes seems that those who are clear and without conditions are not kind to others, their presence alone already helps others and at the same time teaches how to be kind.

Today is the day when seven couples will marry in front of Buddha. I hope that within unconditional love, each of the partners in these seven couples will love the other, and that their partner's presence alone will make them happy and comfortable, so that even if they live together for a long time, they will never tire of one another.

I hope the longer they stay together, the more they will support and give each other happiness, so they will have complete happiness; and I hope that with those happy minds, they become true bodhisattvas who always help others.

815. August 15, 1994. Yun Hwa Dharma Sah

A long time ago in China a master named Sul Du said, "All of the Buddhas and masters never made a Dharma speech for human beings or taught them." What does this mean?

All of the Buddhas and masters appear in order to save sentient beings; that is why they are here. So why did Sul Du say that they never made a Dharma speech for human beings or taught them?

Give me one sentence!

KATZ!!!

The floating cloud which got stuck by the peak of Mauna Kea gives a strong shower to whoever has gotten caught by the five desires. After being showered, the Buddha and master in the red sun greet those who had been caught by desire with smiles of great love and compassion.

How are you today?

816. August 16, 1994. Yun Hwa Dharma Sah

I am trying to write today's teaching, but it seems as though I am only besmirching this white paper. But if I do not write a teaching for today, the day will be uninteresting and dull.

In order to transmit true speech, I must go beyond words and speech. But when I write even one word, I get caught by words and speech.

But there is a moment when I find out how not to get caught by words or speech, as if finding a hole in the net of words or speech.

Ohhh! Hello!

Can you hear me?

Can you see these words?

Thank you!

In the pond, the single lonely lotus flower there blooms and then expands its family — 1, 2, 3…

That is true peace and happiness, and this place is paradise.

817. August 17, 1994. Yun Hwa Dharma Sah

A family comes from true love.

When the members of a family do not understand true love, they do not understand one another and live in difficulty. But when they do understand true love, they understand each other.

Because the members of a family used to love each other, they become a family. But if they do not understand that love, then they are on guard with one another. Then each one expects to be loved by the others and wants to be noticed by them. But if they do not receive that love and attention, they blame and hate each other when they should not.

When the members of a family realize and attain love, all of their blaming, hating and separate actions disappear; they begin to act, think and speak for each other. Then, instead of expecting to receive love and attention from the others, they give love and attention to the others. They finally realize the oneness of family, and realize that in that oneness of family there are no others; all are oneself.

818. August 18, 1994. Yun Hwa Dharma Sah

What is the difference between Buddha's silence and human being's silence? The silences themselves are the same, but in Buddha's silence 10,000 things grow and the flowers bloom. However, the flowers which bloom in Buddha's silence do not have any fragrance.

In human being's silence, not even one flower can live for a long time; whatever grows there soon shrivels. Why is that?

But the day a human being becomes a Buddha, even shriveled plants bear fruit. That fruit becomes a seed; that seed makes 10,000 flowers; and those 10,000 flowers give a beautiful fragrance to the whole world. Why is that?

(silence)

Hmmmm! Yun Hwa Dharma Sah's 100 lotus flowers smell sweet. Hmmmm!

Thank you very much!

819. August 19, 1994. Yun Hwa Dharma Sah

A Buddha is sitting in front of you, but you do not know this Buddha as a Buddha. And so you treat the Buddha just as you would a regular human being.

One morning, however, you realize that this Buddha is indeed a Buddha, and all of your doubting, blaming, anger and jealousy disappear. Then, because you respect and treat this Buddha as a Buddha, you automatically become a Buddha yourself.

At that time, all of your walls disappear and you become one with the Buddha who is sitting in front of you. Then, even though the Buddha does not say a single word and only blinks his eyes, you automatically know what he wants. This brings great happiness for both you and the Buddha sitting in front of you. Seeing the Buddha's dry lips, you offer a glass of water and your own dry lips become moist, too.

But there is a no-Buddha that makes you realize that the Buddha sitting in front of you is indeed a Buddha.

Find that no-Buddha!

820. August 20, 1994. Yun Hwa Dharma Sah (Volcano Ceremony Day)

Dear Fire Goddess: all of the students of Yun Hwa Dharma Sah sincerely bow to you and make offerings to you.

Dear Fire Goddess: always be comfortable, relaxed and tranquil. In tranquility, please become one with Buddha's great love and please find eternal peace.

Today, I will sincerely greet you in Buddha's love. So please let go of all of your difficulties. Please be comfortable so that all sentient beings may also be comfortable and able to practice in comfort, one by one becoming Buddhas so that they may adorn this Buddha land with beauty.

Thank you very much, Fire Goddess. For protecting Yun Hwa Dharma Sah, I especially have sincere appreciation for you.

821. August 21, 1994. Yun Hwa Dharma Sah

Today is the day to be filial to your parents. But if your parents have passed away, it is the day to make a ceremony for them, in order to show your reverence and appreciation for them.

It is because of our parents that we came into this world, and it is through their care, protection and love that we grew up. So let us not forget our gratitude to them. Let us always strive to make them comfortable and happy, helping them with sincerity.

When we were babies, for a long time our parents could not sleep very well at night; later, whenever the family had delicious food and nice things, they always gave to us first. When we were sick, they were fearful and worried about us. Also, they worked very hard in order to be able to give us good educations. They always gave us everything, never holding anything back.

Because we always made our parents worry, we owe them a lot. Even today, I know of a 100-year-old mother who still worries about her eighty-year-old daughter.

In order to show our gratitude to our parents properly, we must practice to become clear, and then with clear minds respond to our parents, understanding their minds and actions. But we should not only treat our parents this way: we should treat all elderly people as our parents, and we should treat all young people as our children. By always making bodhisattva actions for everyone, we can truly pay our debts and show our gratitude to our parents, performing our correct function as human beings.

So sit today for at least three minutes in deep appreciation of your parents, whether they are alive or not.

822. August 22, 1994. Yun Hwa Dharma Sah

Because of one ignorant person, an entire family or group can have problems. It is just like a small stone falling into the quiet ocean and causing many ripples.

When you do not know that someone you live with is ignorant, you also become ignorant and suffer unnecessarily. But if you know that you are dealing with someone who is ignorant, you can exit the cave of ignorance and can see how much suffering that person's ignorance causes.

If you do not want to get caught by ignorant people, first eliminate your own wanting mind; second, eliminate the mind which wants to benefit and only make yourself comfortable; and third, eliminate your ego.

If you do this, even if you do get caught by an ignorant person, you will know how to release yourself quickly. At the same time, this ignorant person will come to respect and follow you, and you will be able to help him come out from ignorance.

823. August 23, 1994. Honolulu

There is an old saying: "When you chop ten times, there is no tree which can remain standing." This means that by putting your mind into something and trying continuously, you will accomplish it.

But before trying, you must be clear about what you really want to accomplish. This way, when you do finally accomplish what you are working toward, you will not have any regrets about it.

For example, in men's and women's relationships with one another, before getting together, prospective partners must see if their relationship is coming from true mind or desire mind. If it is coming from true mind, once established, that relationship will make both people happy and they will not have any regrets. But if it is coming from desire mind, once established, their relationship brings suffering.

However, if a relationship is established through the partners' desires but they nevertheless benefit others, it is a relationship capable of changing into a true relationship.

824. August 24, 1994. Honolulu

The closer your relationship is with someone, the more you should maintain correct manners and respect toward one another. If you do not maintain correct manners and respect toward the person with whom you are closest, this closeness will degenerate into hating and blaming one another.

That is why masters have always said to deal with those closest to you as if for the first time, always thinking of your connection together as being very valuable and special, while treating them as you would a great guest. If you do this, you will become a bodhisattva and will ultimately accomplish Buddhahood.

The closer you are with someone, the more you must make sure not to use one another. Instead of using each other, abide in positions of giving to and benefiting one another. Then you will always enjoy a good relationship and will never be lonely. You will always have an interesting life. In true happiness and with a true smile, you will live every day appreciatively, respected by others, life after life.

825. August 25, 1994. Honolulu

When there is a conflict between people, wise people never listen to only one side of the story. Listening to both sides, they see the whole picture, and are able to judge the situation clearly and respond accordingly.

Unwise people do not know how to harmonize with others. Although they often want to control others, they usually cannot; not getting what they want, they tend to speak badly about others and try bringing other people over onto their own side by being sycophantic and asking for sympathy.

In the face of this kind of behavior, wise people act like lions that do not bite the meat thrown to them, but rather the hands of those throwing it.

Before you judge others, always first be clear yourself and do not get caught by anyone's negative energy. Remember: the wise never speak badly about others unless they have a great reason for doing so.

826. August 26, 1994. Honolulu

When you like and want to make a relationship with someone, the other person must also have some interest in establishing the relationship. If that is so, then a relationship can be made. But if only one person wants to be in a relationship, this brings a lot of suffering both for the person who wants it as well as for the one who doesn't.

If you really love someone and want to have a relationship together, but the other person does not want to be together, then without making that person suffer you should just wish for his or her happiness. If, because of your own feelings, you try to force a relationship, that is not true love; that is desire love. Acting on this desire turns it into jealousy, and that jealousy will poison you.

Truly loving someone is loving without expectations. When you really understand what true love is, your love will always make others happy. But you will not even have thoughts of making others happy; you will just naturally bring them happiness. In this way, you are always receiving and giving love to others without getting caught by your relationship, and you can live a free life, like the wind and the flowing water.

827. August 27, 1994. Honolulu

When we live in the social life, our own work is important but we must also consider and put energy into how to raise a successor. If your work and talent are known only to you and are not taught to or shared with others, then that knowledge and talent will not be transmitted and it will have no lasting value. But when you teach your knowledge and talent to a successor, then that knowledge and talent shine and benefit everyone.

Correct teachers and predecessors find happiness when their successors exceed what they have done. But because unwise people are always afraid that someone else will steal their knowledge and surpass them, they greedily guard their knowledge and talents as great secrets.

Remember, our human life always changes. When you understand the truth of change, no matter what work you do, you will not get caught by anything and you will be able to do your work freely, expertly and without any hindrances.

When water is still it becomes stale. Flowing water performs water's correct function.

828. August 28, 1994. Honolulu

When you chase your desires and live in the desire world, you do not even know that you are living in desire. While chasing your desires, you lose yourself and do not even know what happiness and satisfaction are; you only punish yourself and inflict yourself with suffering.

But one morning you suddenly ask yourself, "Why must I chase my desires?" You realize that in chasing your desires, you made many mistakes and had many fears. Seeing this, you do not like yourself. Not liking yourself in this way is very dangerous because when you give up your desires, you think that you are giving up yourself, and it is easy to fall into a deep hole.

At such times, you must first rescue yourself. In order to do that, try forgetting everything and deeply realizing the value of your present existence, deeply appreciating your situation. Realize the importance of human existence.

The importance of human existence does not lie only in benefiting yourself, but also in profiting others and sharing yourself with them. When you thoroughly realize this, your sentient-being desire changes into bodhisattva-desire; and in this bodhisattva-desire, the lotus flower shimmering with morning dew blooms and then disappears, leaving behind no traces.

829. August 29, 1994. Honolulu

Very good opportunities may come for entering a relationship or undertaking some work, but if you are caught by your own conditions and karma, you cannot be open to receiving or accepting that opportunity. Then afterwards, you experience regret about lost opportunities.

This is like what happens when a wise person brings a thirsty horse to a river full of delicious water, but the horse thinks this water is no good and wants to look for another river, all the time suffering from thirst. Clear people resemble wise horses that only need to see the shadow of the whip to begin galloping forward in the correct direction.

When a good opportunity for a relationship or some endeavor presents itself to those who are wise, they accept it, make it work and are happy with it.

Instead of judging the opportunity which comes your way, practice to be clear so you do not allow that opportunity to pass you by; at the same time, see how much you are caught by your own conditions and karma.

830. August 30, 1994. Honolulu

Those who irritate others always make up reasons for bothering others. When you irritate others, you do not realize that you are actually irritating yourself and that this is the root of irritating others.

Those who irritate others always get caught by their own eyes and ears and do not see or hear the bright world which is beyond the eyes and ears. They think that whatever they happen to be caught by is in fact something correct or true, and by being caught like this, they only make others suffer.

When you want to escape from whatever you are caught by and from whatever bothers your eyes and ears, close your eyes and ears. Then you will not get caught. While keeping your eyes and ears closed, practice vigorously. Then, when you reopen your eyes and ears, everything you had been caught by will have disappeared, and the place where you were caught previously will be full with Buddha's smile. Your face, which was so tight before, will blossom widely and new, and bright eyes and ears will be waiting for you.

Love others 100 percent.

Understand others 100 percent.

Help others 100 percent.

Then that self, so long stuck in the eye of the needle, will see the beautiful, wide world as it is. From this moment, you will never tire from the sound of the dharma birds chirping, and wherever you go you will sleep sweetly and very comfortably.

831. August 31, 1994. Honolulu

Because of your bodily condition, your energy can become tight and you can fall into worry, becoming nervous and fearful. Your bodily condition can also be affected by nature energy. That is why it is sometimes difficult to be comfortable, why your relationships with others can sometimes be uncomfortable, and why your life direction can at times be fraught with many obstacles.

Within the place of Buddha, our body comes from karma and nature energy. But because our bodies are affected by nature energy and karma, sometimes we are not comfortable; and in order to keep our bodies, we must strive and suffer a lot. So at times we have many doubts, such as, "Am I born in order to suffer?"

The place from which we are born is beyond our form-bodies, and yet it makes our bodies. That place is prior to nature's energy, prior to karma. It is the place of Buddha. However, if you say, "The place of Buddha," that is not correct.

If you succeed in realizing the place of no-Buddha, then even if your body condition is not good and nature energy is not tranquil, you will not be hindered by them. Instead, day by day, you will make use of that which is uncomfortable as medicine, and the fact of having a form will become a great happiness. Then, life after life, whenever you have a form body, you will remain still within the place of Buddha, performing your correct functions and duties as a human being.

832. September 1, 1994. Honolulu

Let us have space in our minds and live in it. In our lives, we often get caught by this and that, and cannot truly have mind space. We then easily lose ourselves and make many mistakes for nothing.

Instead of having bright wisdom, within the mind that does not have space, a lot of suffering and fear appear. But when your mind has space, bright wisdom always appears, and within this bright wisdom one creates beauty continuously. That beauty is true beauty, making everyone beautiful. This is called "truly adorning this Buddha land with beauty."

In order to have mind space, try to forget everything. But when you cannot forget something, put whatever you cannot forget into the mantra, and repeat the mantra as much as you can.

833. September 2, 1994. Honolulu

The significance of absolute, present, true human beings is that even if you stay together with them, you do not feel burdened; and the more you stay together, the more joy you have. Such persons do not create even tiny burdens for others and do not make others uncomfortable because of their own feelings. Others hardly even notice that they are present, yet they accomplish all that they must. And even though they accomplish many things, they are reluctant to show that they have done these things. Such persons always benefit others and make them happy.

If you should go on the path with an absolute, present, true human being, you will often have difficulties. The reason for this is that as you go along with an absolute, present, true human being, your own karma appears and is eliminated, bit by bit. It is due to this process that difficulties sometimes appear.

But when the process is finished, you will also have become an absolute, present, true human being and then you will also help others to eliminate their karma. So as time goes by, everyone will become an absolute, present, true human being.

834. September 3, 1994. Honolulu

A truly interesting life is conquering all difficulties. It is when you do not think of difficulty as difficulty, and when you do not neglect those things which are easy. A truly interesting life is also when, every day, moment by moment, you watch each situation as it appears and are not shaken by anything. And it is also when, even though you conquer difficulties, you forget about that which you conquered.

If you can have an unconditional, true, beautiful smile with closed lips, then you will truly enjoy an interesting life and truly realize that life is really interesting.

Remember, we do not come to this world to suffer. We come here to work, and that work is to make the place of Buddha beautiful; that is why we are born here. So while we are alive during this life, let us do many beautiful works. Then, when we return to the beautiful place of Buddha, we can go without any regrets.

835. September 4, 1994. Honolulu

Look at the non-speaking Buddha and *hapchang*.
Look at the non-speaking Buddha and make a vow and a
 wish.
Look at the non-speaking Buddha and show him respect.
If you practice vigorously in front of the non-speaking
 Buddha, you become a non-speaking Buddha yourself.
Look at speaking human beings and *hapchang*.
Look at speaking human beings and make a vow and a wish
 for them.
Look at speaking human beings and show them respect.
If you practice vigorously for speaking human beings, you become a speaking Buddha.

When that speaking Buddha speaks, each word eliminates human beings' sufferings, each word is a guiding light for them, and each word helps make them into Buddhas themselves.

The speaking Buddha speaks but does not speak, and he always keeps himself on the path of the non-speaking Buddha.

836. September 5, 1994. Honolulu

When you thoroughly realize the value of being born and existing, and you appreciate them, you can eliminate your conditions and uncomfortable situations. Then you can understand those situations which made you suffer, as well as those people who bothered you and made you suffer. After these understandings, you will also understand why you came into those situations and why you came into contact with those persons.

Then instead of blaming the people who bothered you and who made you suffer, you will have compassion for them. You will also realize how ignorant you were to blame others and try to escape from your difficult situations. At that time, you will realize your imperfection, and you will vigorously strive to make yourself into a perfect human being.

The blue sky and green mountains are always there. But when your body goes, who will see the beauty of the blue sky and the green mountains? Because your body is here, you can see the blue sky and the green mountains, and you can hear the sound of the birds chirping, and this touches your mind in different ways.

But when your body disappears, who will see and hear those things, and whose mind will be touched?

Ahhh! The sky is blue, the mountains are green, the birds are chirping.

Thank you very much, 10,000 times!

837. September 6, 1994. Honolulu

All human beings are equal. But some people are always given credit and respected by others, while other people are always complained about and brushed off by those they encounter. This happens in social life, family life, community life and professional life.

By abiding by the rules and keeping precepts and vows, people are given credit and become and respected human beings. But those who do not abide by the rules and keep their precepts or vows are not given credit or respected by others, and it is they themselves who cause others to complain about them and brush them off.

Please practice vigorously and become a clear and bright person. Abide by the rules and keep your precepts and vows, but do not get caught by them; find the true Dharma which is beyond rules, precepts and vows. Become one with that Dharma and let us create beautiful social, family, community and professional lives.

838. September 7, 1994. Honolulu

Student: "Dae Poep Sa Nim, I know a chemist who explained to me why Monday is a blue day. The reason is that when they mixed the chemicals together, it was a Saturday, and they needed two days to settle. So by the time they had settled, it was Monday, and the color which had appeared was blue."

Dae Poep Sa Nim: "Ahh. Is that so? But do you know why blue appeared?"

Student: "No."

Dae Poep Sa Nim: "I know why it became blue."

Student: ???

Another student, who was eating his lunch: "So Dae Poep Sa Nim, why did it become blue?"

Dae Poep Sa Nim: "Eat your lunch!"

1) That mind which tries to realize and know why Monday is a blue day is the mind which wants to realize.
2) That mind which explains why Monday is a blue day is the mind which got caught by knowledge.
3) That mind which asks why it became blue is the mind which got caught by blue.
4) That mind which says it knows why blue became blue is the mind which got momentarily caught by its wisdom.
5) That mind which said "Eat your food" is the mind which has no blue, no knowledge, no doubts, no questioning and is not momentarily caught by its wisdom. That mind does the correct function, moment by moment, within the bright and clear place.

When you eat and can just eat, and when you sleep and can just sleep, then blue Monday is interesting as blue Monday, red Sunday is interesting as red Sunday, and everyday is interesting as it is. Then, where are the good days? Where are the bad days?

All of Master Jo Ju's wisdom and functioning are in his cup of tea; that is why he always offered a cup of tea to whoever came to him and asked a question. For his true bodhisattva-action we must have a lot of respect and admiration.

839. September 8, 1994. Honolulu
Do not argue or fight with others.

Instead of arguing and fighting with others, first empty yourself out. Instead of arguing and fighting with others, first lower yourself. Instead of arguing and fighting with others and trying to defeat them, strive to become friends with them.

Also, just because someone is not agreeable to you and difficult for you to deal with, do not run away. Whether your relationship with someone is good or bad, it is because you have a connection together from last life that you met each other in this life. So if you try to escape from a relationship which is not good this life, that bad relationship will continue on in the next life.

If, instead of arguing and fighting with others, you are able to strive to become friends with them, through that mind of striving, the bad relationship disappears; and even if you do not become close friends, the bad relationship karma disappears.

Remember, when you crawl on the ground, there is always someone else who is flying in the air above you, which means when you defeat one person, there is always another one waiting afterwards. So instead of arguing and fighting with others, always strive to be friends with them.

In the mind of striving to be friends with others, there is the power to overcome everything.

840. September 9, 1994. Honolulu

If you are diligent, no matter where you go you will be respected by others and you will live very comfortably. But if you are lazy, no matter where you go you will not be respected by others and you will have a difficult life.

Diligence polishes you, makes you into a correct human being and enables you to shine. It is just like when a rough diamond comes to a correct cutter: the stone becomes beautifully cut, shines and is able to perform its correct diamond function. Meeting the correct cutter is not for someone else; it is for yourself. Do not forget that.

But laziness means that the rough diamond is neither cut nor polished, and so it remains an ordinary stone, does not shine, and cannot perform its correct diamond function; it has a dark life.

Today, lift your tired body out from its tiredness, eliminate its tiredness and work diligently. And remember, no matter what, one's body will always become tired. But the origin of tiredness is ten percent from the body and ninety percent from the mind.

Eliminate all of your delusions, illusions, fantasies, dreams and imaginations and move your present form, now! Move just like a dharma wheel, which rolls continuously.

841. September 10, 1994. Honolulu

When one lies and tries to cover it up, that makes another lie. Later on, it seems that this lie becomes true; one even thinks this is the truth and believes it, and so lie-truth becomes the truth. Then, because that mind strongly believes that this lie-truth is true, others also believe that it is true.

But if there is the mind which does not believe that this lie-truth is true, then this lie-truth cannot become true. And if there were not that mind which wanted to believe in something, then one could not have begun the process of lying from the beginning.

Making a lie comes from small I, and that mind which believes the lie is true comes from ignorant attachment, which creates the seed of suffering. Then one lives as if that lie-I is true I, and when one's body disappears, the body goes but the lie-I cannot get into nirvana; it runs around, and then that lie-I meets a new body and is born again.

P. S. This is a very important teaching. I would like to explain more but I will stop here. Because this teaching may be interpreted in 10,000 different ways, I want you to sit down, meditate and thoroughly comprehend the meaning of this teaching; try to get the true point of what I am explaining.

842. September 11, 1994. Honolulu

Know, but do not know.
Do not know, but know.
Correct, but not correct.
Not correct, but correct.
Thinking this is it; thinking that is it.

Even though we always live in confusion, we feel that there is a place, somewhere, where one knows, where it is correct, and where this is it. So we build up our knowledge and experience. Also, because we would like to find what is beyond knowledge and experience, we would like to find the correct path. So we come to the path of practice, and we practice.

While practicing, you realize why you do not know, why it is not correct, and why this and that are not it. You also realize the importance of practice.

By realizing the importance of practice, you know what the truth is, which is beyond knowledge and experience. Then, you do not get caught by what you know or do not know, by what is correct or incorrect, or by 'this is it' or 'that is it.'

Then, if you do not know, you know that which knows that it does not know; if you know, you know that which knows that it knows; if you are not correct, you know that which knows that it is not correct; and if you are correct, you know that which knows that it is correct. And when this is it, you know this is it; and when that is it, you know that is it.

Then, even though we live in a confused world, you will not be afraid of confusion and you will know how to function correctly in each situation, one by one. You will live an interesting, beautiful life, just as if you were embroidering a beautiful lotus flower without being aware that you are doing so.

843. September 12, 1994. Honolulu

The mind which believes in Buddha (absolute, truth) is the mind which believes in oneself. When one cannot believe in oneself, it is because one does not believe in Buddha.

Believing in Buddha but not getting caught by name and form is true believing. But if you believe because you have been caught by name and form, that is not true believing; that is just an expression of the greed only to save yourself. That greed is the biggest hindrance keeping you from believing in yourself.

In order to believe in yourself, you must first eliminate your wanting mind, do your daily work 100 percent, and practice to not bring delusions into your mind. Then you will begin to believe in yourself, and that believing mind will truly believe in Buddha.

In that true belief in Buddha, you will get what you want, without hindrance or greediness. Also, you will create your life the way you want, and the way you will want your life to be will be what everybody wants.

Doing your daily work 100 percent is saving yourself and others. Then others will believe in you.

844. September 13, 1994. Honolulu

In smartness, there is stupidity, which makes unnecessary ignorance and regrets. In over-confidence, there is a very weak mind, so even if one kills a tiny mosquito, one's heart races. In ignorance, there is unexpected smartness, which surprises oneself and others.

The meaning of these statements is that in strength there is weakness, and in weakness there is strength. So if you are smart, do not try to show that you are smart, and if you are not smart, do not blame yourself for lacking smartness. Always polish yourself, every day, with the practice.

If you are smart, in a smart way become a needed person for others; and if you are not smart, in a not smart way become a needed person for others.

Live without regrets.

845. September 14, 1994. Honolulu

When you expect something but you do not get it, this brings great disappointment. But while disappointed, do not hate or blame yourself and do not blame others.

Being disappointed occurs because your thinking and action are not clear. If your thinking and action are clear, but disappointment comes nonetheless, the significance of that disappointment is that you must realize that you are supposed to do more important and significant duties; it is an opportunity for you to see yourself more fully so that you can make your path clear and correct.

With disappointment, make your path clear and correct.

With success, make yourself humble.

Then instead of cheap tears, diamond wisdom will appear.

846. September 15, 1994. Honolulu

Whatever you do not know, it is good that you do not know.

Whatever you know, it is good that you know.

But when you try to know what you do not know, suffering appears; and afterwards, when you know, you have more agony than you did before you knew. But if, after you know, you do not attach to what you know, you forget it, and do not think about it, you will come to know many things.

Also, when you do not know, but you know what you do not know, attachment, suffering, agony, forgetting and thinking all disappear. Then, without thinking, you know exactly what to do, and you put it into action, now, in this moment. Having done so, you do not doubt your action; you just go forward.

I cannot say that life is not simple.

847. September 16, 1994. Honolulu

Knowing that some people are not so good, knowing that they are trying to use you, that they bother you and need you, you try to push them away. But your mind becomes sore. So then you try to deal with them; but in doing so, you think that because of them you will lose many things and be ruined. So you do not know what to do.

The meaning of having a sore mind when you try pushing such people away is that you have that much affection for them, which is what all human beings should have; affection is the beauty of the human mind.

The meaning of that mind which, as you deal with such people, thinks that you will lose many things and be ruined, is that you are that much unwise.

When you have a lot of affection for others, you often feel stupid and have regrets. But instead of thinking in that negative way, you should be proud that you have that correct human mind, which is the mind people should always have.

And when you deal with others, instead of thinking that because of them you will lose many things and be ruined, think that you exist here in this world, now, so you can have the opportunities to serve others. If you think this way, then in the future the people who tried to use you, who bothered you and made you suffer, will change and become your good friends who really care for you.

But, if worse comes to worst, and those people do not become your close, helpful friends, appreciate the fact that because of them you have had the opportunity to create service karma for yourself. Whoever has a lot of service karma was not poor in their last life and will not be poor in this and future lives.

So if you do not have a comfortable financial situation now, make a lot of service karma.

848. September 18, 1994. Los Angeles

Eliminate everything you get caught by and that bothers you, and go into Buddha (absolute, truth). Then your mind and body will become comfortable, and you can completely relax; you and Buddha become one, and so your yearning and wanting mind disappear.

But when you are in Buddha for a long time, it becomes boring and you miss those things you had gotten caught by and that bothered you in the human world. So you return to the human world; and your comfortable mind, which you had while being in Buddha, disappears. You get caught and bothered again, and you go around in a whirlpool.

At that time, you must realize that you are in that place where you get caught and bothered; you must clearly realize that. Also, at the time, by realizing the place of Buddha, which is comfortable and quiet, you realize that whatever you got caught and bothered by is the real taste of happiness, which you can only have in the human world.

849. September 19, 1994. Paris

While going back and forth in the Buddha world, you meet people you love, people you do not like, people who make you happy, people who make you unhappy, people who make you angry, people who are interesting and people who are not interesting.

While meeting all kinds of different people, you love, you hate, you become angry, you become happy, you become unhappy, you become interested, and you become uninterested. But by realizing the world of Buddha (absolute, truth) and that self which knows the world of Buddha, one does not get caught or pulled by all the different kinds of people, and at the same time one can see and taste the exquisiteness of each person, one by one.

Life seems not to be interesting, but it is interesting. Appreciate that you are here in this human world, and with this mind of appreciation deal with each person, one by one, very importantly. When you deal with people one by one, you do not have fears, and you do not waver; you deal with them as you would your own family. Then, whoever you meet, you feel happy and interested.

850. September 20, 1994. Paris

Let us become loyal people who sustain the loyalty among ourselves and our friends, our families and *sangha*.

Loyal people are always respected and given credit by others. But those who are not loyal and only think of their own present benefit, who act sycophantically towards others and talk behind others' backs, thus making many problems — such people lose respect and credit from others. They are not wanted by others and always raise doubts about themselves.

Though at first it may appear that those who are loyal are not respected or given credit by others, as time goes by they are always respected and given credit by others, and nobody doubts them.

Remember, being loyal to others is actually being loyal to oneself. Loyalty leads one onto the correct path of life, and the person who is loyal will live life without hindrances or blockages, life after life.

851. September 21, 1994. Paris

When you cannot sleep at night, the night seems to be very long. Just so, when there is something you want to accomplish, until you do so, time seems to be very long, and the space around you seems empty and boring. You try to fill the time and space but because you cannot, you feel really miserable.

Even though you want to accomplish something, do not get hung up by it. Until you accomplish what you want, do your daily work sincerely; then accomplishing what you want will come much faster than you expected.

If you do your daily work sincerely, and you do not accomplish what you wanted, that means what you wanted to accomplish was not correct for you. So do not become disappointed at that time; continue to do your daily work sincerely. Then you will not get caught by time or space and you will accomplish what is right for you.

After accomplishing what is right for you, do not become arrogant. Continue to do your daily work sincerely, and then you will go on to accomplish even bigger things.

852. September 22, 1994. Paris

In this clean place of Buddha, according to how you use your mind, your life unfolds.

If you doubt others, you will always live life with doubts.

If you trust others, you will always live life with trust.

If you make others comfortable, you will always live life comfortably.

According to how you use your mind your life unfolds. So always see where your mind goes and before it lands someplace, grab it; wherever you are supposed to use it, use it; and wherever you are not supposed to use it, throw it away. Then the place of no-mind and the place of no-Buddha create beauty. So when spring comes you enjoy the spring flowers, and when autumn comes you enjoy the autumn flowers. Without being preoccupied with either life or death, you create a free and beautiful life.

853. September 23, 1994. Paris

There are those who, the more you stay with them, the more comfortable you become.

There are those who, the more you stay with them, the more uncomfortable you become and you want to leave.

When you stay with those who make you comfortable, your duties and path can easily become unclear. But when you stay with those who make you uncomfortable, your duties and path can become extremely clear.

But if you do not discriminate between comfortable and uncomfortable, and if from time to time, moment to moment, you enjoy in a comfortable way the person who makes you comfortable and also enjoy in an uncomfortable way the person who makes you uncomfortable, then you can make a beautiful flower bloom upon a rotten log, and the fragrance of that flower will penetrate the senses of both the comfortable and the uncomfortable person. Whoever smells the fragrance of that flower will go onto the path of Buddha (absolute, truth, nothingness).

854. September 24, 1994. Paris

While our lives come and go, if we look at life in terms of time and space, it is very short. But while we are here, we often have confused thinking, believing that we will live for a long time. It is even the case sometimes that as people pass away, they do not even realize they are exiting this life.

In confusion we have attachment, and in attachment we have greed and anger, and we easily make ourselves ignorant. That ignorance is ignorance of ourselves, and it causes a lot of unnecessary karma. So often when people go, they go without a good reputation; and when they return, because they are not confident, they return involuntarily by being pulled by their karma.

Once you know this theory, while here you can escape confusion and attachment and walk onto the great path. While walking on the great path, do many things to benefit others and make them happy. Then, while you come and go, without getting exhausted, you will have sweet dreams in Buddha, every single day.

855. September 25, 1994. Paris

A successful person is one who, while in suffering, conquers suffering and comes out of it.

An unsuccessful person is one who, while in suffering, escapes from suffering.

A successful person uses difficulty as medicine.

An unsuccessful person uses difficulty as difficulty.

A successful person understands others.

An unsuccessful person does not even understand himself.

But a person who has attained Buddha (absolute, truth), whether successful or unsuccessful, does not waver and is not hindered by suffering or difficulty. Those who have attained Buddha only go straight; and as they do so, step by step, dharma flowers bloom in their footprints. Those flowers make a dharma-flower crown for both the successful and the unsuccessful people, making them happy and leading them into the place of no-Buddha.

856. September 26, 1994. Paris

Excellent teachers do not show affection to their students. Rather, they demonstrate wisdom for their students so that they can become excellent teachers themselves.

Excellent students do not blame their teachers even a little for not showing them affection. They always appreciate their teacher's teachings, and because they would like to have their teacher's wisdom, they try to conquer all difficulties.

Excellent teachers always strive, without speaking, for their students to have even deeper wisdom than they do. And when a student attains deeper wisdom than theirs, instead of showing their happiness, they purposely make a mistake in front of that student.

Wherever excellent students go, they always credit their teachers by using their teachers' names rather than their own. With bowed heads they always appreciate their teachers' love, compassion and patience.

857. September 27, 1994. Paris

If, because of their personal matters, momentary interests, and wishes to be comfortable, teachers avoid their students, doctors avoid their patients, merchants avoid their merchandise, accountants avoid their numbers, writers avoid their words, and practitioners avoid their practice, then their paths become ruined.

But if teachers are inside of their students and find happiness through teaching, if doctors are inside of their patients and find happiness through curing their sicknesses, if merchants are inside of their merchandise and find happiness through selling the right goods, if accountants are inside of numbers and find happiness through governing the numbers, if writers are inside of words and find happiness through becoming a lover of words, and if practitioners are inside of their practice and find happiness through practicing, then as they travel on their paths these paths shine and are true bodhisattva paths.

858. September 28, 1994. Paris

A long time ago there was a man who knew many people but yet did not have anyone with whom he could really open up and speak truthfully. So he only looked at the moon and spoke with the moon and looked at the sun and spoke with the sun.

One day while speaking with the moon, the rabbit in the moon listened to what the man was saying and squealed about it to the lion in the sun. One half of what the rabbit told the lion was true, but the other half was just his own idea. So when the lion heard the rabbit's story, he became so angry at the man that when he spoke with the sun, angry fire shot out and the man could not continue to speak. And when he spoke with the moon, the rabbit made all kinds of maneuvers so that the man again could not continue to speak.

The man became very disappointed and decided that he would no longer speak with anyone. When the Buddha saw this, he felt a lot of pity for the man. So one night, the Buddha appeared in his dreams and told him, "From now on only speak with me; I will listen to you truthfully."

But the man had become so disappointed that he even doubted the Buddha. The Buddha understood this and told him, "From today close your eyes, ears, nose, mouth, body and mind for twenty-one days. Then you will understand who can truthfully listen to you and who you can trust." Because the man wanted to try one last time, he did what the Buddha suggested.

A very strange thing happened. After twenty-one days his eyes, ears, nose, mouth, body and mind were very open, and he felt so relieved and clear. Strangely enough, whoever he could not trust before, he could trust now. Whoever he spoke with listened to him truthfully, and whoever listened to his speech became his true friend and became very happy.

The man deeply realized that his truth is actually others' truth and that when he is not truthful he makes others untruthful. He was so happy and thankful to the Buddha that he made one hundred and eight prostrations to him; he truly appreciated the Buddha.

859. September 29, 1994. Paris

There is an old saying, "It is difficult to save an unwise person."

No matter how much you teach, no matter how much love you give, and no matter how much you care for unwise people, instead of improving, they always remain at the same level. Because they sometimes seem to be improving, you are very happy. But at those times, it is not that they are improving; it is that their heads are swelling. Their swelled heads are only used to make others uncomfortable. They may believe that they are correct, but that is just their confusion. In confusion, they insist that only they are correct and that all others are not.

Let us practice and practice so that we do not fall into others' ignorance, and let us also strive not to fall into our own ignorance. Whenever you stay with an unwise person, give yourself space; and whenever you are in an unwise situation, give yourself time so you do not make others or yourself suffer. Fill that time and space with practice, let that ignorance become wisdom, and let that wisdom save all ignorant beings.

860. September 30, 1994. Ahaba

When unwise people have a problem, they think they are the only ones in the world who have problems. So they bother others, ask for help from others and present their problem to others; they use up others' time and space and hope this will bring them help. When others do not help them, they complain about them for not doing so.

But when wise persons have a problem they perceive how to take care of it and see why the problem has occurred. By doing so, they find the roots of the problem. After discovering the root causes, they realize that they had become attached to these causes. After realizing this, they find the method of eliminating their attachments, which they realize can only be accomplished by practicing. After realizing this, they practice.

While practicing, they depend upon the Dharma and their master's teaching. Through practicing, they attain wisdom. After attaining wisdom, they realize that their own problems resulted from their ignorance. When they realize this, they drop their ignorance without saying a single word and just go forward, making friends with the blue sky and the wide ocean.

861. October 1, 1994. Ahaba

Those who have a lot of anger inside, but who do not speak about it, have a hard countenance which reveals their feelings. It is difficult for others to look at that kind of countenance.

Those who speak a lot of nonsense, who blame others, who only want to do things their own way and who easily create a lot of anger, have a countenance which is even more difficult to look at.

Because it is difficult to look at such hard faces, you try to neglect or forget them, but you cannot; their ugly countenances and ugly speech remain in your head. When you eat, meditate and so on, their faces and words appear in your mind and bother you; and without your realizing it, they make your own face and speech become hard.

At that kind of time, do not look at others; only see yourself. Then you can see that because of others you got tainted with a stain of negativity. When you see that, strive to forget it. But if it is difficult for you to forget it, do not look at the other person in an ugly way. Instead, listen to the birds singing in the mountains around you. Let hatred and ugly thinking disappear and fill your head with the sounds of the birds singing — chirp, chirp, chirp!!

You can hear the sounds of birds looking for food, looking for their mothers and fighting. No matter how much you hear them, your ears do not become sore and the birds are nothing but cute to you. Then others' ugly countenances and speech will disappear from your mind, and in place of them, another thought will appear, which is, "how can I help that person?"

862. October 2, 1994. Ahaba

When one makes a mistake, that mistake always follows oneself, and that is why we call this 'karma of making a mistake.'

People who have the karma of making others suffer especially receive suffering from others. But after receiving suffering from others, one can eliminate one's karma of making others suffer. It is just like when a child is sick and then afterwards grows more healthily. But if while eliminating the karma of making others suffer, you cannot overcome your own suffering and you only think of yourself, then you create even heavier karma.

A wise person does not try to escape from his or her suffering. Instead, wise people understand that their suffering is a condition of eliminating their karma. And until that karma is eliminated, they practice harder. While practicing, even if they feel they are losing something and that they must do things they don't want to do, they do them and think about how they can benefit others more, going in the direction of benefiting others more than they do themselves. Through this, wise peoples' karma is eliminated, and many people will love, respect and follow them.

It is just like after a tidal wave: the ocean is calm, brilliantly illuminated by the sun shining upon it — a beautiful shining that spreads out everywhere, permeating everything.

863. October 3. 1994. Ahaba

The more experience one has and the older one becomes, the more thinking and doubts and the less faith one has.

But when one's experience and age become really advanced, one's thinking and doubts diminish, and one's faith strengthens.

People who do not practice believe strongly in their ideas and opinions. But practice people strongly believe in practice, the truth and the Dharma. Those who believe in their own ideas and opinions always return to their own karma. But those who believe in the truth and the Dharma always return to the truth and the Dharma.

In the wrinkled face of a person who believes in the truth and the Dharma is a child's smile. But in the wrinkled face of a person who believes in his or her own ideas and opinions is a smile of worry and fear.

Those who have a child's smile wake up by the sound of the rooster crowing in the front of the mountains and go to sleep by the sound of the owl in the back of the mountains. But during the long winter night, those who have smiles of worry and fear rip down 84,000 houses and erect 84,000 houses.

864. October 4, 1994. Paris

In front of someone else, it is easy to compliment that person.
In front of someone else, it is difficult to complain about that person.
It is easy to complain about others, but it is difficult to complain about oneself.
It is easy to cover one's mistake, but it is difficult to cover that mistake of covering.
By trying to eliminate one's mistake, it is easy to make another mistake.
It is difficult to thoroughly eliminate one's mistake.

But wash oneself with love and compassion, understand others, and think of and deal with them just like you are thinking of and dealing with yourself. Then the roots of your complaints and mistakes will disappear. The place where those roots had been will be filled with the fragrance of practice, and in the bosom of the no-Buddha you can comfortably relax.

865. October 5, 1994. Paris

Today is September 1 by the lunar calendar. This is a month to practice and work vigorously, and to receive the results. If you endure difficulties and you practice and work vigorously, then you will receive good results.

Find hope in difficulty, find happiness in working vigorously, find true I through practicing vigorously, and create a new and beautiful life.

Please let this whole month be comfortable, happy and healthy and, furthermore, please be clear.

866. October 6, 1994. Paris

Because you try to follow your lover, it seems as though you are losing whatever you built up in your other relationships, the situations you have, and whatever you have gained from your life experiences. Also, because you do not know what your future with your lover will be, you worry and you have doubts about whether or not he or she will love and care for you forever. But if you try not to follow your lover, you worry that you will lose him or her forever. So because of one lover, day and night you worry about all kinds of things and you make your body sick; you totally distract and often lose yourself.

But remember, a true lover is difficult to find in the midst of desire, greed and lust. So throw away your desire, greed and lust and even throw away your lover, too. Then you will know what true love is. When you know what true love is, your true lover will always be near and you will not have worries or suffering.

A correct relationship exists in the non-interesting place. When you find that correct relationship, you can truly take care of your duties and work on your direction; then your relationship with your true lover can last eternally.

867. October 7, 1994. Rhein Ruhr

No matter how much a person gives you problems and sickens you, when that person goes away, all that is left behind is sadness and a feeling of loss, and whatever he or she did right shines more than what was wrong. That is why the mind of the person who sent him or her away hurts.

There is an old saying, "Even when the moon is full it fades away. So when a relationship is full it also fades away." The sadness you feel when someone goes is greater than the happiness you have when someone comes.

When we come into this world we do many things, but when we leave it we go without saying a word. Yet a person's actions are never erased after going; they always remain behind.

So when you have a relationship with someone, act correctly, appreciate the relation you have together, and love and help one another. Then you will never separate from each other; the good actions you make together will preserve your connection, and you will not suffer the sadness of separation.

868. October 8, 1994. Rhein Rhur

The law of the universe is not complicated. It says:
 Speak, but do not poke others with the tip of your tongue;
 Listen, but forget that speech which bothers you;
 Smell, but do not get enchained by the fragrance;
 See, but do not leave anything left over;
 Touch, but do not leave any marks;
 And act, but act only in order to benefit others.

Doing so, the blue mountain will tell you that without speaking you live very well, and the blue sky will tell you that you live without taint. Anger, desire and greed will *hapchang* and bow their heads to you and, without your needing an admission ticket, the wind and waves will greet and invite you into this life and the next life. You will come and go to and from this world without tiring, living every day happily.

869. October 9, 1994. Rhein Rhur

The speech of those who speak truthfully but not eloquently, word by word and sentence by sentence, will touch others' hearts. The more one listens to their speech, the better and less bored one feels; one feels soothed and relieved.

The speech of those who speak eloquently but not truthfully, word by word and sentence by sentence, is full of knowledge and ideas. Their speech is so smooth, it is like putting oil on a cake, but it does not touch others' hearts. The more one listens to it, the worse and more bored one feels, and after listening one has a bad aftertaste.

True speech does not come from the tip of the tongue; true speech comes from a mind full with love and compassion. One true sentence can pay off thousands of dollars of debt, but Buddha's wordless smile saves all sentient beings.

870. October 10, 1994. Paris

Today, watch how large your ego grows. When your ego becomes big, govern that ego with humility; in humility, watch and keep yourself.

While watching and keeping yourself, if you can forget humility, you can concentrate upon and sincerely do your job 100 percent.

Then the results of your work will shine, will be appreciated and respected by others, and will make them happy.

When you work and have ego, you receive complaints from others. But when you work without ego, you receive love, credit and respect from others.

871. October 11, 1994. Paris

Born HERE, live HERE, go from HERE.

Thinking and vision can reach far away, but everything originates from and is put into motion from HERE.

When thinking is far away, one's mind is not clear. But when thinking is near, one's mind becomes bright.

Putting your thinking HERE, you can see your mind and your thinking. Even as your thinking is appearing, you are able to check it, eliminate what is not correct; allowing only what is correct to manifest, your actions appear out of that correct thinking.

A person who sees HERE sees Buddha.

A person who sees Buddha knows who he or she is.

A person who knows who he or she is truly believes in Buddha and is happy 365 days per year.

P. S. Realize this very important and deep teaching.

872. October 12, 1994. Paris

You always wish for others to become better. But if another person becomes better than yourself, even though you do not show it, jealousy appears. You tell yourself that being jealous is not good, but it appears anyway.

While being jealous, you secretly wish for that other person to fall down. But you know that your mind is going in a bad direction, and so you do not like yourself; you see yourself, and you do not like that you are on such a low level. But you cannot control your negativity, and when you see that person of whom you are jealous, you even become angry.

If you truly wish for others to become better, you should wish that they become better than you yourself. You must make that mind which wishes for others to be better than you appear from no-mind, and you must also return to no-mind. Then you can truly wish for others to be better than you yourself.

Remember, others' happiness is your happiness.

873. October 13, 1994. Paris

Wake-up from ignorance, get away from greed and desire, and see the bright world which is in front of your eyes.

In the bright world without ignorance, greed or desire, everything is full, so you can get what you want, if what you want is for everyone. There, if your greed and desire are also for everyone, it becomes wisdom. But if your greed and desire are only for yourself, they become ignorance, and no matter how much you want to, you cannot see the bright world which is in front of your eyes.

Light becomes light when it shines for others. But if it only shines for itself, it is not light; it is darkness.

874. October 14, 1994. Puchberg

When you are in a difficult situation, it is hard to imagine that a beautiful and comfortable situation exists. But if you are in a difficult situation, treat working through that difficult situation as your duty and carry it out diligently. Then suddenly one day it will change into a beautiful and comfortable situation and you will be so surprised. At that time, you may have a subtle feeling of missing that difficult situation. But your new, beautiful and comfortable situation will be so different that you cannot even express it in words.

Actually, the beautiful and comfortable situation has always been there, but because time, connection and good karma had not yet met together, you experienced difficult situations. It is because you worked and practiced vigorously while in the difficulty, and did not complain, that a good situation could come.

Once in a good situation, you can believe in the beauty and comfort of your situation and can work more diligently and practice more vigorously so that you continuously have better and better situations. You can also truly realize that, beyond your good situation, there is a free and unhindered situation. When you realize that, you can really see that every day is a good day and every day is a new day.

875. October 15, 1994. Puchberg

When people express their opinions to others and find others do not agree with them, they often blame those others for not agreeing and continually insist that they are correct. People like this are only showing that their quantity of knowledge is small.

Before knowledgeable and wise people express their opinions, they listen to others' opinions and, if those opinions are not correct, the wise do not blame others. Rather, the wise explain what is correct, but do not necessarily expect others to agree with them. That mind of not expecting others to agree with one's opinion does not include anger, blame, disappointment or ego.

What is correct always shines, and others automatically follow it. So instead of trying to convince others of your own opinion, convince yourself first.

876. October 16, 1994. Puchberg

Today, make beautiful relations with others. Think of your partner or the person with whom you are closest as the most beautiful person in the world.

Until now, you have gotten caught by your partner's speech and action and thus have been unable to see his or her true beauty. Also, according to what you have been caught by, you have judged him or her, so even though you wanted to see your partner as being beautiful, you could not do so. Because of that, it was difficult for you to have true love for your partner. In one corner of your mind, you always had a fantasy of another person taking the place of the one you actually have. Because that imaginary partner and your real one were not the same, you became disappointed in your actual partner and wished to find a new one.

When you found a new partner, after staying together for awhile you went through the above scenario again, and so you changed your partner many times. While changing your partners you became confused and, because of the karma you created by often changing, you had that much more difficulty in finding your true partner. Finally, nobody trusted you anymore and you became the loneliest person.

So today, think of your partner or the person with whom you are closest as the most beautiful person in the world and as the person whom you truly love. The reason why you meet someone in this life is because of the strong connection you have from last life. So do not forsake that important relationship and create suffering in this life and the next life too.

Now, as of today, make that relationship beautiful and strive to love one another truly. While striving to do that, you will discover true love and you will make a beautiful relationship.

877. October 17, 1994. Paris

Happiness and unhappiness appear because of what you make. When you do not get caught by anything and you are comfortable and clear, happiness is always with you. But when you get caught by many things and you are not comfortable or clear, because of that darkness, happiness does not stay with you.

In order not to get caught by what you see and hear, no matter what others do or say, do not be bothered by it. When you hear and see bad things, forget about them. And when you hear and see good things, even forget about them, too.

When you can forget about what you hear and see, you do not get caught, and you become bright and confident. Then, when you hear and see bad things you know how to fix them, and when you hear and see good things you know how to enjoy them without falling for them.

Happiness and unhappiness do not exist separately; in happiness there is unhappiness, and in unhappiness there is happiness. When you do not think about either happiness or unhappiness, you can always stay in clarity, you can make yourself happy, and you can live every day happily.

878. October 18, 1994. Paris

You know that you are already going onto the correct bodhisattva path and that this is the only path you need to go on. You also know that you are born into this world in order to go onto this path and that you only need to do the work of a bodhisattva.

But while going on that path, once in awhile I, my, me, possessiveness and selfish conditions appear. So you stop along your way, make unnecessary karma, and would like to go onto another path on which you can make your ego grow. Also, you do not want to go in that wrong direction alone, but would like to take others along with you. And when someone does not listen to your idea, you blame him for not doing so.

At that kind of time, always look at yourself; realize that you are not going in the correct direction and practice to eliminate your I, my, me, which are the source of your disturbance.

Because of your small desire, you can demolish your correct path; it is often because of small desires that people cannot go onto the true path and so suffer in the karmic world. So continuously polish yourself, and do not let any wrong things appear which can ruin your true path.

879. October 19, 1994. Paris

Beekeepers are not afraid of the bees; they love them. But in order to reach that point of not being afraid of the bees, they must strive to learn how to handle them, and they must endure being stung many times and being sore. But finally, beekeepers conquer their fear of the bees, and through their striving and suffering they come to know about bees and their value, and come to love and respect their togetherness and mind of loyalty.

Also, the bees are moved and impressed by the beekeepers' non-tainted love and endurance, and so they come to trust and follow their keepers.

Once you realize the meaning of this and then deal with difficult people, you have endurance and patience; you can make yourself clear without any taint, and you can give true love to others. Then, the difficult people follow and appreciate you.

880. October 20, 1994. Paris

When you eat food which is too delicious, it tastes good but it is not so healthy for your body. It is the same with people: when you first meet a person who is very interesting and good, at first you like being with him or her, but as time goes by you have many headaches.

When you eat food which does not look or taste too good, it is often nourishing and healthy for your body. It is the same thing with people: when you meet a person who does not seem to be too interesting and whom you do not like too much, as time goes by, more and more that person helps you and you have good feelings and love for him or her.

But there is also food which looks and tastes good and which is nourishing for your body. It is also the same thing with people: there are people who are interesting and who, the more you spend time with them, the more comfortable you are, the more they help you, and the happier you become.

When those who are awakened deal with others, whether they are good or bad people, they deal with them equally. However, they deal less with those people who are very good and with whom they are most comfortable.

881. October 21, 1994. Paris

There are humble people who work hard, but who never say or think that they work hard.

There are people who do not work hard, but who say and think that they work hard and who even want to give their work to others.

If you think of your work as work, it is work; and before you even begin, you want to escape from it. But if you do not think of your work as work, but instead think of it as part of your path, as what you must do, and as your life, then it is not work; it becomes very interesting, and the more you do, the more excited and interested you become, and the more experience and abilities you have. Your work becomes you, and you become your work. Then you do not feel tired and you are always given credit by others and earn their respect.

Also, while working in this way, you can make your own true vacation. During that vacation, you can work truly, just like the Dharma wheel which never stops turning; while moving and working you can have a true taste of life, every day. Then, when you go to Nirvana you can really enjoy it.

882. October 22, 1994. Paris

There are people who, even though they are far away from you, seem to be near. There are people who, even though they are close by you, seem to be far away. And there are people who, the more you spend time with them, the better you feel.

You have a feeling for those who are far away but who seem to be near, and the more you think of them the more comfortable and warm you feel, and you would like to be with that person all of the time.

No matter how much you would like to be close with those who are close by, but who seem to be far away, you cannot connect with them; when together, you feel uncomfortable and burdened, and your thoughts are not of them but rather go in a different direction.

You have too much feeling for those who, the more you spend time with them, the better you feel; you feel too good with them, and so it is easy to forget about your work and direction.

When you deal with others, do not let yourself be too distant or too close, and do not let yourself fall for them too much. When you are with someone, just appreciate being together and deal with all people equally. Then missing others, having difficulty with others, and falling for others will all disappear, and you can concentrate upon your duties and direction correctly, every day, in a bright and clear way.

883. October 23, 1994. Paris

When you lose others' credit and care, and your position too, do not become angry or disappointed. Instead, strive to build up and improve yourself. Take your experience as your practice. Through striving hard, you will regain others' credit and care, and you will earn a better position than the one you lost.

Wise people did not gain their wisdom in one morning, and the flower that bloomed under the rotten log was also not able to do this in a single morning. Taking difficulty as your teacher and finding wisdom through difficulty is especially true for the bodhisattva path. Your wisdom derived from facing difficulty will shine upon others, take away their troubles and save them.

There is one sentence in the great bodhisattva vow: "I will take upon myself all sentient beings' difficulties until they no longer suffer." I hope you know what that means.

884. October 24, 1994. Paris

When a cat exposes his claws and wants to fight, not even a lion can conquer that energy, so the lion walks away.

When somebody does not trust you, no matter what you do, that person does not like it; they find small faults in everything and constantly bother you. When in that kind of situation, instead of trying to win over such people, take space from them for awhile, and practice and polish yourself until right wisdom appears.

When you attain right wisdom, however, do not run to those who made you suffer or think you will save them. By thinking you will save others, your ego grows, and then the wisdom you attained cannot be bright. But when you are in bright wisdom and you think of others as yourself, with no-ego and no-wisdom you can transcend trust or distrust, like or dislike, taking space or not taking space, and you become one with others. Then, within equality, together you enjoy peace.

885. October 25, 1994. Paris

The three poisons (desire, anger, ignorance) matter when you are young. But when you become old, instead of the three poisons, what matters is your wanting the three comforts (living quietly, having good digestion, sleeping comfortably).

The three poisons and three comforts matter when you are alive, but when you die you throw those things away like old shoes. But the box (karma) in which you kept the three poisons and three comforts follows you, and next life you return within the same box.

Practicing people eliminate the three poisons and three comforts, and when they come into life and pass away from it, they do so without a box, as they wish, in the wide and clear space. However, until all others' boxes disappear, they come and go without resting, and in joyful tiredness they live every day appreciatively.

886. October 26, 1994. Paris

In the entire universe, the most beautiful place is this planet.

In the entire universe, the most interesting life is human life on this planet.

In the entire universe, the happiest life one can have is living on this planet.

The meaning of us being born as human beings, and on this planet rather than another is:
1) That we have a great deal of good and beautiful karma from the last life.
2) That we had a vow to help each other.
3) That we had a bodhisattva mind and a mind of sacrifice in order to make each other happy.

That is why we are born on this planet. But because of being reborn again, we forget these facts and:
1) We do not know what true beauty is.
2) We only want to live for ourselves.
3) Because of ourselves we bother others.

This is why it is difficult to live an interesting and happy life, and why we live in suffering and then pass away.

Practice people: thoroughly understand the meaning of this and do not dirty this world because of yourselves. Rather, do bodhisattva actions and find no-I. In no-I, find love and compassion, become one with love and compassion, and live every day beautifully.

887. October 27, 1994. Paris

When you are very hungry and you eat a lot at one time, you get indigestion. Also, if you usually eat too much each day, you get indigestion.

It is the same thing with work: when you work too much at one time or too much in one day, your body and mind become exhausted.

But each day do not be lazy. During the week, work diligently. Then on the weekend, check what you did that week. That way you can see whatever mistakes you made and you can be careful not to repeat them. Also, forget about whatever you did well.

During the weekends, or on your days off, practice harder. Then more correct wisdom and methods will appear for you, and the following week's work will be interesting and will have very good results. Your work becomes you, you become your work, and whatever you do you will be secure and confident. Then you can do your work very well, you will be respected and credited by others, and you will be a truly needed person for them. You can also easily bring out all kinds of talents from yourself which will benefit and make others happy, and which will also bring a rich and fruitful life for you.

888. October 28, 1994. Paris

Find beauty while living this present life.

Beauty is always here, but because you cannot get away from the world of attachment, you cannot discover the world of beauty. In order to get away from the world of attachment, forget whatever you are attached to as much as possible and become a non-self. Going from the world of attachment to the world of non-attachment is very difficult. That is why Shakyamuni Buddha did a lot of ascetic training when he practiced for six years.

While going from the world of attachment to the world of non-attachment, it sometimes seems as though you are losing your human life. But when you thoroughly attain and realize the world of non-attachment, not even one thing is not beautiful and your 10,000 doubts, suspicions, questions and everything you had while in the world of attachment disappears. Then you know what true beauty is. With that beauty you help, benefit and lead others onto the correct path, living your life without taint.

When you think that you are suffering, be happy that you are going away from the world of attachment; when you think that nothing is interesting, be happy that you are going into the world of non-attachment; and when you become beautiful, be happy that you have become a Buddha.

889. October 29, 1994. Paris

Forget about whatever mistakes you made in the past; when you begin anew, everything becomes new.

Do not carry what is past into the present. When you do your best today, your past mistakes become your teachers, and tomorrow they will become good teachers for others. Also, the more you forget whatever good experiences you had in the past, the clearer you become, and the more you can do your best today. Then you can appreciate the present and create it beautifully.

The creation of beauty comes from the bright and clear place. But if even one thread gets caught in the process of creation, then the result is not a true creation, but only a copy. A copy comes from the world of opposites; but a creation comes from the world of the absolute.

When you meet a Buddha, you learn the Dharma to become a Buddha yourself. After you attain the Dharma, you have to throw away that Dharma. Then you can become a Buddha, and that Buddha can create the Dharma beautifully. That beautiful creation makes beautiful history which will be retold to others in the future and will make everyone beautiful.

890. October 30, 1994. Paris

Often, the more time you spend with a certain person, the more difficulties you have with him or her. You would like to be free from that person, but sometimes you cannot because of the situation. So you have a lot of hardship. Also, the more you think about what he or she says and does, the worse you feel; you may even wake up while sleeping at night because you continue to think about it. Because of that thinking, you cannot even have a light, pleasant morning.

This kind of situation often appears in relationships; but actually, it is not that the other person is making you suffer. Rather, because of him or her you can see your own mistakes and lack of clarity very clearly. And, because you do not want to see that truth and would like to avoid it, you have a lot of difficulties, which shows how many faults you have. At such times, try to forget everything and think of that difficult person in a loving way, just as though you are loving yourself.

When the roof of a house is not well made, rain leaks through it. So practice harder in to keep the three poisons (desire, anger and ignorance) from coming into you. Then that difficult person will become your favorite person.

891. October 31, 1994. Paris

The human personality has some very interesting aspects.

When a hurricane suddenly comes upon a calm ocean with small waves, the waves become very large and rough. Similarly, interesting things sometimes occur in quiet human minds. At certain times, those things are suddenly activated and cause you to do things you cannot explain and afterwards regret. This is due to particular parts of one's karma being activated.

Your knowledge, experiences and age obscure that karma. But when you are in a very comfortable situation with no worries and everything is going smoothly, that karma can be activated. So from time to time, when you cannot control that karma, it appears and causes you to become angry and irritable for no apparent reason. Then, both you and others suffer.

This explains why people who are in a happy situation often worry and are scared they will lose their happiness, and why a very nice person can suddenly and unexpectedly act in a very strange way. But practitioners are able to control their karma through practice before it can be activated.

So always watch yourself. If your karma is activated sometimes, correct your mistake right away and practice regularly so you can eliminate your karma and live without any regrets.

892. November 1, 1994. Paris

The path of practice is the right path.

Though at the beginning and middle of one's practice, there are always obstacles which can keep you from continuing on the path, if you are certain that the path of practice is the right path, you can transcend those obstacles. But if you have doubts about the path of practice and are not clear that it is the right path, those obstacles pull you into a whirlpool of suffering and you forget about the path. However, after experiencing many difficulties, you finally realize that the path of practice is the only correct path and that it alone can save you.

Other paths proceed hand in hand with the three poisons (desire, anger and ignorance) and the five desires (for food, fame, sleep, sex and money), and keep one wandering about and subject to the eight sufferings (being born, becoming old, becoming sick, dying, not getting what you want, being separated from those whom you love, being with those whom you dislike, and imbalance of the five skandhas or elemental constituents).

But through the path of practice one comes to know the meaning of the Four Noble Truths (suffering, the cause of suffering, the end of suffering and enlightenment), one polishes oneself with the six paramitas (the paths of perfecting offering, keeping the precepts, forbearance, mindfulness, practice and wisdom), one becomes one with the truth and true-I, and becomes an absolute, free person.

You will thoroughly realize in your bones the magnificence of the power of practice, and regardless of how many temptations and obstacles come your way, you will be able to push them aside and on this path only practice and live every day in a true paradise. You will also thoroughly and truly appreciate the path of practice; you will thoroughly and truly appreciate your teacher who teaches you the practice; and you will thoroughly and truly appreciate the *sangha* in which you practice.

893. November 2, 1994. Paris

The desire to possess others and have things for yourself only enslaves you and makes you suffer, and your feelings and affections only make you weak.

Whoever has a lot of desire is not free, and whoever has a lot of feelings and affections has many tears. But a wise person's desire is to practice, to be with the truth, to bring others to the truth, to make them truthful, and to bring everybody into one, true family. The wise therefore give themselves to the truth and, through their feelings and affections, understand what each person needs and what makes them happy.

That is why the wise find freedom in being together with many people. Also, through their great desire, everything they do becomes successful, they have great appreciation, and even though they do not have their own personal time, a vacation, or a day off, they relax and enjoy their time with others.

894. November 3, 1994. Paris

There once was a carpenter who was employed to build a house. When he looked at the wood which was supplied, he saw a twisted piece and said, "This wood is twisted, so I cannot use it." Then he saw a jagged piece of wood and said, "This piece is jagged, therefore I have no place for it." The next piece he saw was bent and said, "This piece of wood is bent, so I cannot use it either." He tried to find pieces of wood which he liked, but could not. So he felt very exasperated and stopped working.

Because of this, the person who had employed the carpenter fired him and hired another one. When that carpenter looked at the wood and saw the twisted piece, he said, "This wood is twisted, but I have somewhere to use it." When he saw the jagged piece, he said, "This piece is jagged, but I know where it will be perfect." And when he saw the bent piece, he said, "This is bent, but I have just the right place for it." He enjoyed working very much and easily built a beautiful house. Everyone was very happy with his great achievement, and he became famous and rich and lived very happily.

A person who has many conditions and who is very negative and pessimistic is like the first carpenter; and a person who eliminates his own conditions, who adjusts to others' conditions, and who is very positive and optimistic is like the second carpenter.

Now, today, which carpenter are you like?

895. November 4, 1994. Munich

It is hard to overcome your difficulties and obstacles through your talents, abilities and knowledge; in order to overcome them you must have the faith that you can do so. However, if your faith is strong and you overcome your difficulties and obstacles, but you do not have the support or protection of the truth and absolute energy, then you become arrogant and create new obstacles. But if your faith comes from the truth, and you overcome your difficulties and obstacles, you do not think that those were difficulties or obstacles or that you conquered them; you only think that you did your duty. So if the more difficulties and obstacles you overcome, the more humble you become, those difficulties and obstacles do not reappear.

The purpose of faith, which comes from the truth, is to benefit others and to make them happy. You should therefore put all of your energy into helping others overcome their difficulties and obstacles and live every day in an appreciative way.

In order to attain true faith, one must practice.

896. November 5, 1994. Munich

This mind is actually Buddha.

Whoever sees this mind knows how to use it correctly and so is actually Buddha; but whoever does not see this mind only understands what mind is through his or her own karma. For those who see this mind, it is possible to transform their karma. Creating correct karma, they know what their path is. Because they know this, they know everything and only create bodhisattva karma.

In no-mind, everything exists through the no-Buddha, and that Buddha through which everything exists becomes one with the person who uses no-mind. That is why this mind is Buddha and why Buddha is this mind.

So where is this mind now???

Today is November 5th. The morning sun is shining and it makes your face pink like a beautiful flower. Please be comfortable all day long.

897. November 6, 1994. Munich

There is true beauty in your mind, but until you can go into that true beauty and become one with it, it is difficult to have true relationships or to connect with others. When you find true beauty and realize what it is, then you can overcome relationship difficulties and you can truly love, connect with and become one with anyone and live beautifully together.

In order to attain true love, you must first let go of your conditions, become one with no-Buddha and find Buddha's jewel in no-Buddha. When you can use Buddha's jewel without hindrance to create whatever you want, then you can find true beauty. That true beauty makes everyone's six senses (the eyes, ears, nose, tongue, body and mind) and six dusts (color, sound, smell, taste, touch and objects of mind) bright, and it eliminates their three poisons so that this present world can become nirvana and paradise and can make everyone beautiful.

898. November 7, 1994. Paris

Although you try to understand others' conditions and to do whatever they ask of you, some people ask too much, and so you become annoyed with them and try to avoid them. But you cannot avoid them all the time. When you think of them, you feel uncomfortable; and when you see them, you feel even worse. You do not want to listen to them, you would like to forget about what they ask you to do, and the more you see how many conditions they have, the more you would like to avoid them.

Then one day in a quiet and peaceful moment, while practicing you completely relax and forget everything. Then those people you did not like suddenly appear and, to your surprise, you do not feel hatred or unfriendliness towards them. You realize that there are understandable reasons for their conditions, that your own conditions were actually stronger than theirs, and that this is the real reason their conditions seemed to be so burdensome to you. For this reason you became annoyed and could not connect with one another.

It was difficult to let go of your conditions, but through practicing you did so; and because you were able to accept those other people's conditions 100 percent, they became very happy and appreciative of you. Because they also came to understand and accept your conditions, you felt ashamed of yourself. So those whom you disliked before and whom you kept at a great distance became your closest, most trustworthy and lovable friends, and you finally realized the power of being unconditional.

899. November 8, 1994. Paris

You practice in the whirlpools of the ocean of desire and make a row boat out of the practice. No matter how much the boat rocks while making headway, you are not scared and you have great faith that that boat is the only thing which can save you from the ocean of desire. So you row on vigorously, and as time goes by the waves become calm and, without even realizing it, the boat eventually comes to rest upon the seashore.

When you get out of the boat you feel very comfortable and happy. But that comfort and happiness are only momentary because when the bright morning sun shines upon the ocean of desire, you see very clearly that your family, friends and all others who are in some way connected with you are still suffering in the ocean. When you see that, you cannot continue relaxing there on the shore, by yourself.

So you get back into that boat which you thought you no longer needed and row again into the rough waves. But, to your surprise, it is not as difficult as it previously was; without rocking, the boat goes effortlessly as if someone else were rowing it for you. The boat picks up the people one by one who are suffering in the ocean, and each time it becomes full, it drops them off on the shore of happiness.

Today, tomorrow and every day, without resting, that boat will continuously go back and forth between the shore and the sea until not even one person remains in the ocean of desire.

900. November 9, 1994. Paris

If one does not always know which work has priority in one's job, one becomes ignorant, loses the esteem of one's boss and may even lose one's job.

Sometimes employees think that they have too much work to do, and so when their employer asks them to do another task they tell their boss that they cannot do it and to please ask someone else. People like this cannot succeed in their work, lose the respect of their boss, and fail in their job because they are caught by their own conditions.

However, no matter how much work those who have eliminated their own conditions have to do, they do not complain and work very diligently. Through working diligently, they accomplish many things; and the more they work, the greater their abilities become, and they soon attain the wisdom of working correctly. Because they are esteemed by everyone, they eventually become bosses.

901. November 10, 1994. Paris

As your practice deepens, your sight and other senses become clear. What you could not see clearly before you can now see clearly; and what you could not feel clearly before, you can now feel clearly. That is why, for example, you previously thought that a certain person was very good in all respects, but now you can see his or her faults. And that is why, having previously condemned another person because you thought he or she was very bad, you now understand why the person behaves incorrectly.

When your senses become clearer, you must practice harder because you become much more sensitive than you were previously; if you are not bright and do not have a strong center, you easily get caught by what you see and hear. You then suffer. Until you are bright and your center is strong, avoid as much as possible whatever will upset and perturb you, but overcome through practice those things and situations which are unavoidable.

Then those situations to which you felt very susceptible will become calm and bright, clear wisdom will appear; then when you are in a situation that must be dealt with in a strong way, you will use that wisdom in a strong way, and when you are in a situation that must be dealt with in a mild way, you will use that wisdom in a mild way. You will no longer suffer or lose yourself in those situations, and you will transform every situation into a beautiful situation.

902. November 11, 1994. Frankfurt

When wise horses see the shadow of the whip, they immediately begin to gallop in the direction their rider wants them to go; but unwise horses do not move even when whipped.

When trying to make unwise horses move, do not become angry; instead, be patient and imitate them by acting like an unmoving horse, too. Then they will think you are a stupid horse. They will laugh at you while starting to move and tell you to start moving yourself.

Do not become angry even when such horses smirk at you; just follow them. Since they do not like to be followed, they will then gallop away. When they do so, leave; go your own way and forget about them. Then you will be able to see the blue sky, the green mountain and the red flower, and you will be able to smell the fragrance of the lotus blossom.

903. November 12, 1994. Frankfurt

Everything in this world is created and balanced through *yin* and *yang* energies. When *yin* and *yang* are balanced, everything is at ease and there is much prosperity. But when *yin* and *yang* are unbalanced, everything is difficult and bad things happen.

There are some people who, the more time you spend with them, the more at ease you become; and there are other people who, the more time you spend with them, the more ill at ease you become. Before and after you began to practice, those difficult situations bothered and affected you. However, as your practice deepens, you cease to be distressed or affected by them; and even if you are in a situation where *yin* and *yang* are unbalanced, you have the wisdom to adjust yourself to that unbalanced energy.

Through wisdom one is always able to create correct karma and correct relationships. While going on one's path, one meets the right people, one is not hindered by *yin* or *yang*, and one does not forsake those true relationships; one always lives with the right people.

904. November 13, 1994. Frankfurt

When you have a problem, your mind is ill at ease, and whether you eat, walk, sit or work, you are unsettled. You become cranky, almost crazy, and you lose interest in living because you direct all of your energy into the problem. You would like to find a method of solving your problem, but you become very exasperated because you cannot do so. Even if you meditate upon the problem, the solution does not appear.

Even while seeing the blue sky and the blue ocean, the problem remains suspended in front of you. But then you remember that the master said, "When you have a problem, forget it." So you try to forget it. But the more you try, the more thinking appears, and you really suffer. Then, in that moment, the mantra appears and you say to yourself, "The mantra is connected with the truth and all methods appear from the truth, so in order to connect with the truth I must believe in the mantra and I must repeat it energetically."

After repeating the mantra energetically, what is in front of you is clear, the wisdom to solve your problem appears, and you greatly appreciate the mantra's power.

Thank you very much!

Na Mu Kwan Se Um Bo Sal,
Na Mu So Ga Mo Ni Bul,
Chong Gak Mio Poep Yon Hwa Kyong.

905. November 14, 1994. Paris

Today, let us show our deep appreciation for Buddha's (the absolute's, the truth's) great love and compassion. With our mind of appreciation, let us wash away all our ignorance and let us become one with Buddha and perform our human duty correctly.

We are born on this planet to create beauty. So let us think beautifully, speak beautifully and act beautifully so that we can make others beautiful and turn this world into a beautiful Dharma flower garden.

Let us transform this world into a paradise so that whoever comes here in the future can really relax and live happily in great prosperity.

906. November 15, 1994. Paris

Nowadays, some married couples suffer from certain problems, the main one being that of the man going off with another woman. This problem is a result of nature's unbalanced energy and the change of seasons. Men's physical energy is very strong in the autumn and winter and they must know how to use it correctly so they can avoid doing something they will regret afterwards.

If a man cannot control his physical energy, he falls prey to sexual desire; because of that, he can lose his family, friends, job and everything he has, thus becoming a lonely person.

Rescue yourself from your desire and live life correctly so that your life does not become lonely. Old shoes are very comfortable, and when they need repairing, you can fix them so that they are like new ones; but completely new shoes make blisters on your feet, so although you try to wear them, before long you remove them and go barefoot.

The grass always seems to be greener on the other side of the fence, but that is not so; make your own grass greener and more beautiful.

907. November 16, 1994. Paris

Let us be people who are esteemed by others.

Let us be people who are needed by others.

Let us be people who are loved and respected by others.

Even if you created a lot of negative karma in previous lives, if you can control your emotions and desires in this life, if you are thrifty, and if you care about others' comfort more than you do your own, then through your great efforts you will eliminate all your negative karma. Then your present and future lives will be bright and you will be sincerely invited by all sentient beings to return each life. You will always be reborn in a good place, you will be a leader or a teacher, and you will carry out your responsibilities sincerely.

908. November 17, 1994. Paris

You do not have to try to know others. If you want to really know others, then strive to know yourself. When you realize and know yourself, you will also know others.

When you realize yourself, others become you. So when others are happy, you are happy; when others are sad, you are sad; and when others are comfortable, you are comfortable. You always put all your attention and energy into making others happy and comfortable and into bringing them onto the true path. Your practice for others never ceases, and through it you find happiness and come to fully appreciate your life.

When your mind is tranquil, my mind is tranquil.
When your mind fluctuates, my mind fluctuates.
Tranquility and agitation are tied together,
And on the no-path path,
With one glass of no-white white wine,
You feel relaxed and satisfied.
Not seeing or hearing anything, this place is paradise.
Hello dear! Please relax.

909. November 18, 1994. Paris

Eat appropriately.
Sleep appropriately.
Practice appropriately.
Work appropriately; and when you have a lot of work to do,
    work hard but do not overwork.
Relaxing is always relaxed.

When you eat, eat in a relaxed way.
When you sleep, sleep in a relaxed way.
When you practice, practice in a relaxed way.
When you have a lot of work, work with a relaxed mind and then you will not feel tired.

When you go on vacation, relax your body, but try to bring your mind very close to Buddha (absolute, truth). When you become one with Buddha, you will know how to eat correctly, how to sleep correctly, and how to practice correctly. Then your work is not work; it is your duty and function, and the more you work, the more interested you become in it and the happier you are.

910. November 19, 1994. Paris

When you really do not know, but believe that you do, that is like walking on a path in the middle of the night under the shine of a wolf's eyes.

When you truly know, but pretend that you do not, that is like walking a moonlit path as easily as if it were daytime.

If you can sincerely do your 100 percent best moment-to-moment, without distinguishing between knowing and not-knowing, then you can go at night under the shine of the bright, round moon and during the day under the shine of the bright sun, traveling the shadowless way. That way is bright, wide and open; it does not have agonies, thinking or hindrances. The footprints of those who go on this shadowless way become guiding lights for others so that they can follow comfortably.

This way that is no-way is the Dharma path. Traveling this Dharma path makes sentient beings beautiful and enables everyone to help turn the great Dharma wheel so that they, too, can go happily together upon the path.

911. November 20, 1994. Paris

Within love... but desperately searching for love.
Within fire... but desperately searching for fire.
Within Buddha... but desperately searching for Buddha.
Love does not know that it itself is love.
Fire does not know that it itself is fire.
Buddha does not know that it itself is Buddha.
But, when love loves, it knows what love is and calls itself love;
When fire burns, it knows what fire is and calls itself fire;
When Buddha does Buddha actions, it knows what Buddha is and calls itself Buddha.

Putting something into action, you can accomplish it; but when you do not put something into action, you do not know what it is and cannot accomplish it.

Putting your behind on the cushion and sitting for a long time does not by itself eliminate your karma, and does not by itself turn you into a Buddha. Sit and meditate as is appropriate, but also move, undertake many actions, and find true I (Buddha) through those actions.

912. November 21, 1994. Paris

When your practice has deepened, while sleeping at night, you wake up a few times, see and check yourself, and discover new wisdom. However, because that bright and clear wisdom does not appear during the day, you forget about it. This process is repeated many times.

As time goes by, your practice deepens further and you begin remembering your nighttime insights and wisdom during the day and begin acting wisely; you become an awakened person both daytime and nighttime.

Because those who are awakened see and know everything clearly and brightly, they do each thing very clearly and effectively, and so people who follow them receive correct guidance and teaching and live comfortable lives without fears. Those people then also become bright and clear and help others in the same way.

The eyes of an awakened person see with tranquility, but the eyes of an ignorant person see with fear.

Those who practice relax their bodies at night by sleeping, but their minds are always bright and clear, even while sleeping.

913. November 22, 1994. Paris

As nature's energy becomes more unbalanced, it has more effect on human beings' energy and makes them more vulnerable. When people whose energies do not balance stay together, unnecessary difficulties arise, it is hard to settle the energy between them, and they easily become uncomfortable. This is why, in many Asian traditions, when people meet and interact with one another, they check if *yin* and *yang* energies balance between them. If their energies do not match, then their opinions conflict and it is difficult for them to harmonize together.

However, for wise people, whether their energy matches with others' or not, they do not enter into conflict. The wise know how to adjust their energy to that of others and so have no hindrances in interacting with them.

Today, if there is a person with whom you think you do not match, have a cup of tea or coffee together.

914. November 23, 1994. Paris

It is difficult to find your own abilities if you want to depend on others or have them help you. Being like this renders you incapable — a person who is not needed. But if no matter what comes your way, you strive to do it, taking care of your own responsibilities, you discover your own abilities, find yourself, and do your job correctly. To be like this is to become a needed person for others.

There are those who cannot do their jobs correctly but who nevertheless act as though they have the abilities to do so, thus making many mistakes, bothering others and making trouble for themselves.

When wise people do not know how to do something, they always ask others. But they also retain responsibility for their own actions and duties; they do not rely upon others and always try to find their own abilities. When they do, they use their abilities freely and become needed persons for others. Their situations and positions are always secure, they become secure persons, and they live their lives without fear.

915. November 24, 1994. Paris

When people you adore or like make a mistake, you still adore or like them as they are. But you cannot adore people you dislike, no matter how much good they do; you just do not like them. Even if you would like to deal equally with all people, it is difficult to do so and you feel uncomfortable and bothered. In this situation, it is difficult to free yourself. But if you do not get caught by people you adore or by those you dislike, if you deal with each person individually and in a cherishing way, and if you appreciate meeting and being together and the connection you have with one another, then you think of each person as yourself. Then, should you be with people you dislike, you can correct your own mistakes; and should you be with people you adore or like, you can diminish your desire and ego. Indeed, if you can treat your long-time friend as though you have just met one another, and if you treat someone you just met as an old friend, then you will not be caught by adoring or disliking; you will be able to deal with everyone equally and free yourself.

916. November 25, 1994. Paris

Today is a day during which to practice vigorously and find correct mindfulness.

Practice and I become one.
Find I in the practice; and in the I, find true I.
That I then finds out how to think and act,
And without doubts or questions, thinks and acts as it is.
While practicing, question what I is.

Then that question and doubt, and even the thought that you are practicing, disappears.

At that time, I becomes practice, practice becomes I, and I becomes one with practice.

Practicing, that I finds no-true I, and this true I becomes one with I.

So when that I thinks and acts, everything is accomplished, and these accomplishments are always in accord with the right and complete path.

The right and complete path is the Eightfold path: right or complete views, thoughts, speech, karma, life, practice, mindfulness and meditation.

917. November 26, 1994. Paris

The birth of human beings into this world is a great joy for humankind and for everything. Through being born, they obtain a new life. They should not waste this opportunity; they should strive to live with appreciation, finding happiness and beauty. After finding happiness and beauty, when they can give everything to others and leave this life without having any expectations or wanting anything, then they will create yet more new lives and will have great joy in being reborn, life after life, eternally.

With new bodies and lives, they will live to help others and make them happy, just as Shakyamuni Buddha did 2,500 years ago upon finding happiness and beauty. Continuously since then, the Buddha has been offering that happiness and beauty to others through continuously changing forms.

I sincerely congratulate those of you who have been born into this world. Happy birth-world to you all!!!

918. November 27, 1994. Paris

The meaning of receiving precepts is making one's direction correct, putting one's scattered self into one place, polishing and making oneself shine, and carrying out one's function 100 percent correctly.

There is an old saying: "If there are more than 300 precious stones, they must be put together in order to become jewelry." The self which was scattered around is put into one place through receiving the precepts.

Keeping the precepts eliminates whatever is incorrect about oneself and polishes and makes oneself into jewelry. This polished jewelry then carries out its function and makes everyone happy and beautiful.

The mind which decides to receive precepts sets one on the path of making oneself into jewelry. That path is always protected by absolute energy, so from the day you receive precepts you can go forward without doubts or fears, doing your daily function 100 percent. That path is the path of becoming one with Buddha, the path of appreciation through which you can have the true taste of human life.

Congratulations to those of you who received precepts today!

919. November 28, 1994. Paris

As one's practice deepens, one's energy becomes very sensitive and one's senses function more clearly and correctly. So when one deals with others, one knows what their energy, personality, and actions are like and even what their thoughts are. You must be careful at this time, because when you are with a person who is very negative and whose thoughts and actions are not good, you can be affected a lot. When dealing with that sort of person, you can become angry and upset unnecessarily, and you can easily become dirtied.

As your practice deepens, you must always be careful about meeting others; try to avoid difficult people so that you do not lose yourself, and practice harder. But when you are with a difficult person whom you cannot avoid, repeat the mantra to yourself and deal with that person just as if you are dealing with yourself.

920. November 29, 1994. Paris

The person to whom you give special care and love gives you special disappointment. Your expectations become greater because you give special care and love to someone, and you wish that this person had the same intention you do. You even wish for this person's intentions to be better than your own, but when your expectations are not met, your disappointment is great.

When you give love and care to everybody equally, you do not become disappointed. However, the human mind does not always work that way. When you want to give special love to someone and you do not want to get disappointed, then do not have any special expectations and just care for and love that person without conditions.

If you want to give special love to someone, then give more and greater love without expecting anything special in return.

The importance of love is in giving rather than receiving.

921. November 30, 1994. Honolulu

When the master leads a student to the correct path, the student knows it is the correct path but still wants to go in a different direction; so the master lets that student go wherever he or she wants. However, when the student goes in the direction he or she wants, the things the student wished for do not come true. So the student comes back and follows the path which the master suggested. But the student still may not really appreciate the master's suggestion and may suffer and feel sad.

When masters see their students suffering and experiencing sadness, they have doubts about their suggestions and regret having brought their students to conduct themselves in the correct way. At the same time, masters think they should have pushed harder to give their students what they wanted, even though that would have carried them in the wrong direction. Because of this, masters sometimes cannot sleep very well at night, and so they practice harder and check themselves to see whether or not their suggestions were correct for their students. But when masters practice harder, they see that what they suggested was indeed clear; so they help their students continuously until they let go of their sadness and suffering. As time goes by, students finally realize that what they wanted was not correct, and ultimately they eliminate their sadness and suffering, follow the correct path, and live very happily.

Seen from the outside, teaching and guiding others seems to be very easy, but it is not; one must strive and practice in order to teach and guide others.

Remember that there is great sadness behind the smile of the Buddha who is sitting very quietly.

922. December 1, 1994. Honolulu

There is an old saying: "One small, dirty fish can dirty the whole fish tank." This means that one person's ego, greed, desire and unclear mind can bother others and dirty the clean and beautiful place. People like this often confuse others and may even separate people and make them complain about each other, thus causing them to make bad karma. Such unclear people become angry very easily, talk in a bad way to others, speak with one person one way and with another person another way, telling tales on them and making them unable to harmonize together.

People like this act and talk as they do because they were like this in their last life. Even though they practice, habits of acting and talking this way easily appear, often without them realizing what they are really doing. However, as their practice deepens, people like this begin to see and control themselves. They begin eliminating their habits and can even transform their bad karma into good karma. Therefore, even bad people can become good people with a bright future who, instead of bothering others, help them to become good people also. This is the power of practice.

So practicing people, do not disparage others just because they are bad; and do not like others too much just because they are good. Make your mind wide as space so that you can deal equally with everyone.

923. December 2, 1994. Honolulu

You live in the beautiful place, but because you are covered by your own karma you cannot see this beauty and cannot live beautifully; yet you regret it when you leave the beautiful place and find you can no longer have the opportunity to live beautifully.

Practice vigorously, open your eyes, which are covered by your own karma, see beauty, and strive to live beautifully; while striving, you automatically speak, act and think beautifully, and you become a beautiful person. You can then live beautifully in the beautiful place all the time, and you can share your beauty with others, enabling you to perform true, bodhisattva actions.

In beauty there is complete freedom, peace and happiness. When you realize and see this beauty, you can become a Buddha yourself and will be able to lead a true human life. Human beings' original place is beauty. So the significance of your being born into this world as a human being is to create and use this beauty freely, and to create beauty wherever you go. By doing so, you carry out your correct function as a human being.

924. December 3, 1994. Honolulu

Do not handle anger with anger.

Do not handle jealousy with jealousy.

Do not handle badness with badness.

When anger is handled with anger, then through that anger one becomes anger.

When jealousy is handled with jealousy, then through that jealousy one becomes jealousy.

When badness is handled with badness, then through that badness one becomes badness.

Handle anger with tranquility.

Handle jealousy with time.

Handle badness with goodness.

Then the roots of anger, jealousy and badness disappear; lotus flowers bloom in the place where those roots had been, and their fragrance makes everyone into Buddhas and bodhisattvas.

925. December 4, 1994. Honolulu

Do not worry if your body is fat, thin or short, or if your face is not beautiful. You cannot say that a person is beautiful just because he or she has a beautiful form. No matter how nice-looking a person's body is, if his or her speech and actions are not beautiful, then instead of seeing that person as beautiful, others see him or her as unattractive. However, if his or her body is not nice-looking but his or her speech and action are beautiful, then others see that person as beautiful and attractive.

Each morning when wash your face and brush your teeth, do not only wash your body; also clean your mind so you do not speak in ways which others dislike and do not act in ways which bother others. Speak and act in ways which help others; then your present form, which you received according to the karma you created in your previous life, will become beautiful and you will receive the kind of form you want in your next life.

A beautiful mind creates a beautiful body.

An ugly mind makes a beautiful body become ugly.

926. December 5, 1994. Honolulu

When you conduct business, just conduct it as business.

If while conducting business, you indulge in a love relationship and get caught by it, then it is difficult for that business to succeed; and even if it does succeed at first, it will soon fail and that love relationship will also fail.

When we use energy, we must concentrate it in one place; when it is focused in one place, then that focused energy accomplishes whatever it is you concentrate on. However, if while concentrating in one place you try to attend to other things, then none of those things will be accomplished.

There is an old saying, "A person who has had difficulties and then succeeds in his business and lives well can easily stop concentrating on the business, indulge in a love relationship and get caught by it, and then lose the business, his or her family, and even that love relationship." The more one succeeds in business, the more sincere one must be in one's business and with one's family, and the more careful one must be not to succumb to external seductions. One must practice regularly so that one can continue to be successful forever and live happily.

Check yourself today:

Are you in a situation in which you are succumbing to external seductions?

If you are a married person, are you loyal to your family?

Are you practicing correctly?

See yourself today.

927. December 6, 1994. Honolulu

Do not lose respect for the person you are very close to. Sometimes when you spend time with a person you are very close to and he or she is very nice to you, you view that person disparagingly. Therefore, when you receive credit from others, you must be careful not to become arrogant.

As a tree grows, it provides shade for others, and even after being made into timber it makes others comfortable and happy. The more successful and important human beings become, the more they must take care of others. By doing so, they become true human beings and fulfill their correct human functions.

The more knowledgeable you are, the humbler you should be. That is true beauty.

928. December 7, 1994. Seoul

Some people live in this world very stylishly and beautifully, and then they depart.

Some people live in this world with worries, and then they depart.

Some people live in this world with disappointment because their wishes are never fulfilled, and then they depart.

If we want to live stylishly and beautifully in this world, we must see Buddha (absolute) which is in front of our eyes and must truly realize Buddha. Doing so, we can create our lives as we wish, living stylishly, interestingly, happily and then departing when appropriate.

When we can live in this world in a stylish, interesting and happy way, we realize beauty. That beauty is not for us only. It will lead everyone to the *maha banya paramita* and will save everyone from suffering.

929. December 8, 1994. Seoul

All human beings are at the same level. But according to their education, background, wealth and capability they are treated differently. When someone has a better education and background and is wealthier and more capable than you are, you feel intimidated without realizing it, and that makes you lose your freedom. And when someone has a lower education and background and is not as wealthy or capable as you are, you become arrogant.

Intimidation and arrogance make you suffer and lose your freedom. Therefore, when you see a person who is better than you, instead of being intimidated, respect him or her; and when you see someone who is lower than yourself, instead of being arrogant, truly help him or her to become better than you are. Then you can live freely in the world of the equal, true I and can create beauty and live happily.

930. December 10, 1994. Seoul

See what direction your mind is going; and if you have precepts, see whether or not you are keeping them.

Today's energy is unclear, and on this sort of day one's mind easily enters the desire world and the karma world. Because *yin* energy is especially strong today, all the nuns should remember that you are nuns and eliminate the three poisons (desire, anger and ignorance);

also remember that you became a nun for the great, big family, and try to eliminate your personal emotions, feelings and ego.

Today, nuns must repeat the mantra 50,000 times and do 500 prostrations. Remember that nuns have the responsibility and duty of being everyone's mother or sister.

Besides the nuns, today all women who have precepts must repeat the mantra 10,000 times and make 300 prostrations. Today, let all ladies attain clarity, be beautiful lotus flowers, and share this beauty with others.

931. December 11, 1994. Seoul

Although you must follow your own path, when you are in a crowd of people you easily get pushed here and there, and you tend to forget your path. Later, you end up in the wrong place and you regret it. However, if you are clear it does not matter how many people there are, and even though you get pushed here and there, you do not forget your direction; instead, you arrive at your destination and you accomplish your goal.

There are always obstacles and hindrances when you have a goal you want to reach; but when you are clear, you will be able to overcome whatever obstacles and hindrances appear and reach your goal. Always practice to be clear, and from today refrain from expecting not to have any blockages or hindrances along your path; instead, rescue yourself from whatever blockages and hindrances appear.

The lotus flower which blooms in the dirty mud is more beautiful and has a more beautiful fragrance than the lotus flower which blooms in the clean pond.

932. December 12, 1994. Seoul

Human beings live at many different levels; for example, some people live very well and other people live very poorly. While everyone wants to live very well and they try hard to do so, not everyone succeeds. No matter how hard they all try, people who live well, live well; and people who live poorly, live poorly. It seems to be unfair.

If you want to live well and try hard but do not succeed, it is because your way of trying is not correct. The correct way of trying is to clean one's mind first. If you only think of yourself and your own benefit, if you make use of any and all methods to benefit yourself, and in so doing hurt others, though at first it may seem you are accomplishing what you want, the results of your action eventually hurt you.

This is why the Buddha said to become rich by making a small profit, and to be satisfied with a small profit. If people use even a small profit for others, they will always receive the karma of being rich; and even though they do not want anything, they will always live a wealthy life.

933. December 13, 1994. Honolulu

When one first goes onto the path of Buddha it seems as though that path is not interesting. But as time goes by, everything becomes smooth and everything which is accomplished is very fruitful.

Those paths which are not the path of Buddha are paths of desire. When people strive on the path of desire, it appears as though they accomplish what they desire; in the end, however, desire culminates in more desire, and so all their efforts and time are wasted.

When one first goes onto the path of Buddha, it seems to be very difficult because of one's individual karma; but when that period passes, whatever was not interesting becomes interesting and one realizes the meaning of true interest. One can then create a truly interesting life and can enjoy it; that is why in the sutras it says to find interest in that which is not interesting.

Desire is just like rough water's foam, but truth is always truth. The path of Buddha is the path of truth. True I, which is in the truth, always truthfully protects oneself. That is why the path of Buddha is always comfortable, why it accomplishes everything smoothly, and why, by being on it, one can live truthfully and comfortably.

934. December 14, 1994. Honolulu

All human beings are the same, but according to one's individual karma, situations and circumstances, one may be a good person or one may be a negative person. Do not like people just because they are good, and do not dislike people just because they are negative. Respect good people, but put more energy into and give more love to those who are negative, just as you give more water to nourish a shriveled flower than you do a healthy flower.

No matter how bad or negative a person is, there is good truth in that person's mind. In order to bring out that goodness and truth, we must offer the truth; then he or she can bring out goodness and truth. But if you label negative people as completely bad, then your own mind's door will close, you will make your mind bad, and you will become bad.

Do not make such discriminations as "they are good, but these others are bad," especially in regard to people who are related or connected with you. Just strive to help them and bring them into happiness. When you strive and put your energy into making others happy, you are actually making yourself happy.

935. December 15, 1994. Honolulu

If smart people act smart, they are not smarter than those who are not smart. Because of their smartness, they ruin themselves. It is as though they put themselves on a lonely island and make their lives like those of frogs, each living all alone in a well.

Even if some people have five or ten doctoral degrees, if they try to act or be smart, then they do not have faith in themselves; furthermore, they will not find the true I — that in which they are supposed to have faith. Because they do not know what true I is, all of their degrees enchain them, keeping them not free, separating them from others.

However, should they realize true I, find great love and compassion, which are in true I, and begin acting truly with love and compassion, then their doctoral degrees become everyone's doctoral degrees and they help others to live in a stylish and beautiful way.

Shakyamuni Buddha's doctoral degree is just like the Dharma, his actions are the Dharma wheel, and those actions save and help everyone.

936. December 16, 1994. Honolulu

Today, try not to be nervous and try to be tranquil.

There are many things in social life which can make you nervous. By trying not to make a mistake you become nervous. After making a mistake you become nervous about the effects of your mistakes. Because you do not want to get hurt by others, you become nervous; and because you want to protect yourself, you become nervous. All of these ways of becoming nervous cause you to become stressed, and that stress makes you unclear. So the more nervous you make yourself, the unhappier you become.

Do not worry about whatever you did in the past or about whatever has already occurred.

Today, practice to become tranquil. In tranquility, find true I; becoming one with true I, do your daily work, one thing at a time, in a comfortable and relaxed way. When you can do your work, one thing at a time, in a relaxed way, nervousness disappears; your work becomes interesting, and that interest makes you comfortable, happy and truly satisfied.

937. December 17, 1994. Honolulu

The significance of being a couple is, "*il shim dong che*," which means, "same mind, same body." People become a couple in this life because they made a strong connection together in their previous life, even though they may have initially been strangers to one another last life.

When partners realize the importance of the relationship and connection which they have with each other, when they keep that relationship correctly in this life, and control one another's emotions and desires, then two people become one and they can be a true couple. A husband sacrifices himself for his wife and a wife sacrifices herself for her husband. When you have this kind of bodhisattva mind and you live for others, you can be a true couple. Marriage is not business; it is to give one's truth to one's partner. Therefore, when a person marries because of his desires and feelings, it is not marriage; it is suffering.

Truth appears when you and your partner strive to give yourselves to one another. That truth becomes one mind, and that one mind becomes one body. Then you live truthfully and beautifully for your family and for everyone.

Especially married couples should remember the sentence, "*il shim dong che*." Same mind, same body.

938. December 18, 1994. Honolulu

Always settle your excited mind when you receive invitations to parties. Wherever you go, go with a settled mind; then you will not get whirled about by the situation, you will not lose yourself, you will not speak or act unnecessarily, you will not have any regrets afterwards, and you will also not get caught by the party after you leave it.

Always speak and act beautifully with a settled mind so that everyone who interacts with you will happily greet you in a respectful way, and so that after parting from them they will compliment you to others.

Especially during holiday seasons, always think about the world of Buddha (the absolute), tranquility and clarity so that you can make others happy. And if you are not clear, then dance with the mantra.

939. December 19, 1994. Honolulu

Do not become disappointed if you express your idea but it does not resonate with other people. Instead of being disappointed, check your idea to see whether or not it was clear. If it was not, do not become angry or disappointed; just forget about it.

A clear and bright idea always relates to and connects with others, even though it may take some time to do so. An idea must originate from the bright and clear place. If it comes from ego, knowledge and karma, then it is not a clear and bright idea; it is only your opinion. Opinions always come from the world of opposites, and that is why they are always caught between agreement and disagreement, connection and disconnection.

Without putting opinions into it, the world of the absolute, which is Buddha's world, is truth. Truth is always relevant to others. Having ideas without opinions is the purpose and intention of Buddha. So create ideas within the place of no-thinking.

940. December 20, 1994. Honolulu

A secret becomes a secret when you keep it as a secret. When you want to know some else's secret, you become excited and you have difficulty. But after you know the secret, it is actually nothing exciting.

There are two kinds of secrets. The first kind appears because you try to keep the truth. In the truth there are no secrets, and you want to let others know the truth. But because sometimes they cannot digest it, you worry that they may suffer if they know the truth. So you cannot tell them because the time is not correct.

The second kind appears because you would like to hide a lie. But a truthful secret is nothing, and in realizing nothingness, the secret disappears.

If you want to know secrets, you must realize nothingness. When you realize nothingness, you will know all secrets; and after you know them, there is nothing to catch or hinder you. Then, on the white sheet of paper on the table before you, you can draw a big smile which makes both you and others laugh.

941. December 21, 1994. Honolulu

People usually think that happiness is when their wishes are fulfilled or when someone loves them. But true happiness is when, with good health, you are in the place of no-thinking and everything automatically goes into the correct path; when the people to whom you are related or connected become very good, go onto the correct path and do their correct function; and when a person does very well because of your help. That is true happiness.

Happiness is not just for yourself; it is for everybody. When everyone is happy, you are happy. And when others are not happy, but you are, you feel very insecure and fearful. So others' happiness is your happiness, and your happiness is others' happiness.

Please be happy today.

942. December 22. 1994. Honolulu

Two people argue because they are alike. If one of the two is better than the other, or if one of the two is wise, then they would not argue. Trying to defeat others through arguing is ignorant. So before you try to defeat others, you must eliminate your ignorance. When ignorance disappears, wisdom appears. Then you do not fight with anyone and you do not even create the kinds of problems that lead to fighting.

Those who put themselves one step lower than others instead of one step higher do not get caught by fighting or arguing. In the quietude, they shine, are respected by others, and without any fighting come to be better than others. Those who can live and depart quietly do not get caught by samsara and live truly free lives, life after life.

943. December 23, 1994. Honolulu

If you want to believe someone else's speech 100 percent, you will be disappointed. But if you can believe what others say 80 percent, then you can trust and believe in those people.

Twenty percent of what people say is just decoration, like frosting on a cake. Therefore, before you blame others for not speaking truthfully, blame your own ears and clean them, because your ears hear what they want to hear and do not hear what they do not want to hear. If you want to listen 100 percent to what others say without getting caught, first strive to trust your own ears. If you can trust your own 100 percent, then even if others say things you cannot trust, you can trust those people 100 percent; and at the same time, you can show them and make them realize how to speak truthfully.

944. December 24, 1994, Honolulu

Today is Christmas Eve, so let us give sincere congratulations to Jesus Christ for his birth.

Shakyamuni Buddha and Jesus Christ were born in this world in order to save all sentient beings, and according to their wisdom and methods they guided and taught many people. So let us sincerely respect and hold in high esteem their great intentions. We should not discriminate in relation to their teachings, judging them as being good or bad, right or wrong. Instead, let us know their true intentions.

In order to know their true intentions, we first must depart from the world of opposites. When we depart from the world of opposites and see them from the world of the absolute, they are all great bodhisattvas who came to this world to save all sentient beings.

All sentient beings come from the world of the absolute. We are one family. So we should all give great respect and bow to whoever is saving sentient beings in this world.

Also, do not only get caught by the shinning lights on the Christmas tree. Find your own mind's shinning light, and with that light let us all together save the myriad sentient beings who are suffering in this saha world.

945. December 25, 1994, Honolulu

The higher and more important your position becomes, the easier it is for you to lose yourself.

The reason for this is that your ego becomes bigger. Your thinking about 'I' and about your conditions becomes stronger. You may think that by doing this, you have found yourself and must protect yourself. In actuality, you will be losing yourself. And having lost yourself, you become the loneliest person.

The higher or more important your position becomes, the humbler you should be. You should change your thinking about your own 'I' into thinking about others. You should also respect their thinking and give more importance to their conditions than you do to your own. Then you become truly clear, your 'I' becomes clear, and you can earnestly and sincerely commit to others and work for them, for your family, your work and your society. Respected by many people, you can become a needed and important person for others and can enjoy and appreciate life forever.

946. December 26, 1994, Honolulu

It is difficult for people who have a lot of desire or wanting mind to have smooth relationships with others, and the amount they want is the very amount they suffer.

However, as their wanting and desiring mind gets smaller, they can have smooth relationships with others. The more their wanting mind diminishes, the more they know who they are, and the more they realize what they should do.

When they realize what they have to do, disliking a person and liking a person disappear. Then they can deal with everybody equally without any hindrances. And yet, when they deal with good people, they give them great respect; and when they deal with not-yet-good people, they give them compassion.

Their own wanting and desiring mind changes into the mind which wants everyone to become good, and that mind of wanting everyone to become good gradually becomes as big as an ocean. And whenever they use that big, wide mind, they accomplish everything without wanting and without suffering.

Everything goes into the correct path without leaving any traces.

947. December 27, 1994, Honolulu

A true party and true interest are in your own mind. If your own mind is comfortable and does not have any hindrances, then wherever you go and whoever you meet will be interesting and you will open up; you will make a happy party, and you will make everyone happy. You will open the closed mind doors of whomever you meet so they can have more space and more time. This action will help them to eliminate the agonies and worries they have gotten caught by.

So, before you meet anybody, strive to make your own mind comfortable and empty yourself out of whatever you have gotten caught by. Then you are ready for others. You can become a truthful host or hostess for others and your truthful smile will make the dark shadows on their faces vanish.

948. December 28, 1994. Yun Hwa Dharma Sah

Enlightenment means that you drop all fighting with the agonies, worries and obstacles you have met in the course of the day. Coming home, you put your head on your pillow and relax. While relaxing, you think about how you can make the people you used to know and the people who are related to you comfortable and happy. Right away, you forget the right and wrong of whatever external problems and situations you had, you forget hatefulness and temptation, and you just go through each thing, one by one. You try to make each situation a happy one, bringing out the beauty of each situation without experiencing any hindrances in it. You make others one with you so there is no distinction between you and them. Forgetting "you" and "I," in togetherness there is only seeing the beauty of the lotus flower and being filled with its fragrance.

949. December 29, 1994. Yun Hwa Dharma Sah

When the wise have a discussion with others, they accept everything which is discussed in a positive way, find out what is right and what is wrong, and respect others' opinions before they express their own. Wise people always have smooth discussions with others and bring out correct results.

When unwise people have a discussion with others, they always engage everything in a negative way and say that their own opinions are right. Therefore, they are not respected by others, do not reach agreement with others, and are brushed off.

The purpose of having a discussion is to put everyone's opinion into one place and thereby benefit others. Then, even if there is an incorrect opinion that everyone initially agrees with, it can be rectified. So when you have a discussion with others, always discuss in a quiet way without I, my, me. Be like a small drop of water which falls in one place and gathers there with others to become a great river flowing into the wide ocean.

Always have patience and follow what is flowing; that way we can eliminate arguing and can accomplish everything in a tranquil way.

950. December 30, 1994. Yun Hwa Dharma Sah

The number one taste in the world is the taste of practice.
Of all the joys in the world, the joy of the Dharma is number one.
When all desires and lust end, all suffering ends.

Strive to find the Dharma and practice it. Then suffering becomes your teacher who governs desire and lust. Brought into the Dharma, desire and lust become a Dharma flower that makes the path of practice more beautiful. Without taste or fragrance, this Dharma flower makes everyone exquisitely happy.

951. December 31, 1994. Yun Hwa Dharma Sah

Today is the last day of you, Dog Year. During your time, there were many good and many bad situations. But through practicing, the bad situations changed into good situations, and the good situations were shared with others. Since there were no essentially bad or good situations, we are comfortable in sending you off, but even so we feel nostalgic for you. Still, we know that we are going to see you again in sixty years, so saying the word "good-bye" is clear.

Sixty years from now, name and form will be different, but that mind which will see and meet you again and that mind which sends you off now are not different. That mind truly wishes that sixty years from now many people will become Buddhas and bodhisattvas and will greet you.

With this wish in mind, before our eyes, the Buddha's face, which has great love and great compassion, is full with a smile.

Suddenly the pig in front of the door squeals.

"Happy New Year!"
"Gul, gul, gul."

www.ingramcontent.com/pod-product-compliance
Lightning Source LLC
Chambersburg PA
CBHW022003160426
43197CB00007B/255